MORE MONEY

WHEN I TRIED TO MAKE MY FIRST MILLION, IT ENDED IN KIDNAPPING AND BLOODSHED.

JASON SHIFRIN

Published by John Blake Publishing Ltd,
3 Bramber Court, 2 Bramber Road,
London W14 9PB, England

www.johnblakepublishing.co.uk

www.facebook.com/Johnblakepub   facebook

twitter.com/johnblakepub   twitter

First published in paperback in 2011

ISBN: 978 184358 418 6

British Library Cataloguing-in-Publication Data:

A catalogue record for this book is available from the British Library.

Design by www.envydesign.co.uk

Printed and bound by CPI Group (UK) Ltd, Croydon, CR0 4YY

1 3 5 7 9 10 8 6 4 2

© Text copyright Jason Shifrin/Wensley Clarkson

Papers used by John Blake Publishing are natural,
recyclable products made from wood grown in sustainable forests.
The manufacturing processes conform to the environmental
regulations of the country of origin.

I would like to dedicate this book to:

My wife, Nicole, for standing by me through all the hardship I have caused her. She is my backbone and the love of my life. My children, Arabella and Jacob – they have been my inspiration for writing this book. Their love has given me the reason to get through this chapter of my life. I love you both. My mum and dad, Peter and Barbara Shifrin – words cannot express how sorry I am for putting them through hell and back, and yet they still continue to be there for my family and me. I thank and love you very much. My sister Amanda and her family – Pier, Naomi, Daniel and Ben – for always being there to support me. My Booba (Hilda Gladstone), a true example to learn from and a wonderful lady who I love very much. Aunty Hazel, Uncle Mike and Aunty Maureen. My cousins Andrew, Lee, Lara, Julian and Elliot. Special thanks to Elliot, who calls me every day and is always trying to help me. My friends – Elliot and Lucy, Nicola and Brandon, Darren and Justine, Darren and Alison, Mark and Lucy, Lance and Victoria, Caroline and Ashley, Big Paul and Leslie, Don Charles, Les Ade, Adrian Whitson, Simon Gilbert, Brian and Rose, Marc and Katharine, Simon, Abi, Charlotte and Oily, Steve and Elayne, Simon Dalli – and all my other friends and family. Without your help and support it would have been impossible to get through the hard years. I have pushed you all to the boundaries but you have all stayed there for me. Thank you.

In memory of my Nanna and Pappa, Michael and Ann Shifrin, my Zida Sid Gladstone (who I had a special bond with – I miss you every day), Uncle Arnold Gladstone, my brother in law whose life was cut way too short, Stephane Tafel.

I am truly sorry to all the people who believed in me and who I let down. I hope this book will help you understand what was going on in my world; there are many bridges to rebuild and I hope I get the opportunity to do so.

The names and identifying characteristics of some individuals portrayed in this book have been changed.

'Ya know they always say, if you live in one place
long enough, you are that place.'
Rocky Balboa

CONTENTS

INTRODUCTION

I am in deep shit to the tune of nearly £10 million and I cannot find anyone to bail me out of this hole, not even my old family friend Alan Sugar – back then it was Sir – or Lord Sugar, to give him his proper title. No one wants to give me the time of day and yet I've got myself into this mess because I genuinely believed that I could be as successful as my boyhood hero, the star of TV's *The Apprentice*. Alan Sugar was my inspiration as a child and I tried to learn from his incredible success but, in the end, it all collapsed like a house of cards.

This is not some predictable true-crime tale by yet another so-called 'notorious hardman' because, essentially, I am nothing more than a happily married businessman surrounded by a close-knit group of family and friends, including the Sugar family. But the chilling truth about how I have strived to keep myself financially afloat is a real-life horror story that should stand as a lesson to any would-be entrepreneur, who thinks that it really is as easy as it appears on *The Apprentice*. I tried to take the business world by the scruff of the neck but, instead, I've ended up with half of London's gangsters on my tail because I owe them all money, and lots of it. Financially speaking, I am nothing more than a time-bomb just ticking away, waiting to explode … and it's fucking scary. Now, not even my old family friend Alan Sugar will help me get out of this mess.

I am writing this book in the hope that it might perhaps put others off ever getting themselves into the same sort of hole I now find myself in. If, God forbid, I end up dead before this book is published, then at least I can say that this is how it is. This is what it's like if you let your finances spiral completely out of control.

Only recently, I had a very unfriendly 'visitor' call at my house who wanted to 'remind' me about some money I owed him. I remember my young son woke up later that same night and called for me and I gave him a cuddle and, when I asked him what was wrong, he looked up at me very sadly and said he'd had a dream that I had died. He was just seven years old and he knew I was in danger. That shook me to the core.

I desperately want to lead a normal life with my wife and family but, for the immediate future, I have no choice but to duck and dive through the badlands of east London and Essex, paying one debt collector with a loan from another. It's a vicious circle of deceit, for which I only have myself to blame.

When I was at school, I wanted to be an actor. I always had this urge to be famous. I avoided getting beaten up by the hardnuts at school by making them into my best friends. I thought that attitude would work in the real, adult world. I couldn't have been more wrong.

My favourite film of all time is *Rocky* and I used to dream of being just like Sly Stallone's character, taking on the world and making myself a fortune through nothing but sheer determination and hard work. I loved the way Rocky was the underdog who wasn't meant to reign supreme and yet he won the world championship. That was how I used to see myself, until the vultures began circling and picking me off, bit by bit.

The message from *Rocky* was loud and clear: if you really want things in life, you have to go out there and get them. My parents didn't particularly encourage that sort of attitude when I was growing up so I had to develop it for myself. Maybe that's where all my problems began. The odds against winning the National Lottery or *X Factor* are huge, but, if you never have a go, you'll never find out.

It's ironic I should use that sort of betting analogy because I'm not even a gambling man. I don't do drugs either, or drink much. Money is my drug and it's definitely caused my downfall.

Part of my problem was that I didn't really fully appreciate the trouble I was getting into until it was all too late. I grew up in a safe, sensible environment where people didn't go to the police because they never needed to. In any case, you'd be seen as a grass, so I pushed all my problems under the carpet as if to say 'tomorrow will never come and something will get me out of this'. Of course, it never did.

Let me give you a brief insight into what it's like to be late with an interest payment if you take a 'loan' out from a criminal. First of all, your life is threatened. Often, that money is owed in turn to another gangster who is invariably the sort of character who'd drive straight through your gates in his Range Rover and then snatch one of your children.

Until recently, I'd kept all this away from the people I love. Or at least I tried to, until my two worlds began to collide. Obviously, I didn't want to involve my family in the seedy underbelly of the world that I had entered in order to borrow money. On the surface, I was leading this impressive, respectable life filled with untold riches. I was trapped by my own obsession with 'keeping up appearances'. But more of that later.

People always say that honesty is the best policy, but it isn't really. If I was teaching kids at school now, I'd say, 'How can you prove that honesty is the best policy?' If someone is standing there with a gun to your head, you are going to tell them what they want to hear, *not* what is the truth. It's obvious. I should know, because I have been at the other end of a barrel or two in recent years.

Let's face it, people always say they wish they knew the truth but most people can't handle the truth when it is staring them right in the face. Look how people often react when you tell them the facts. Most of them don't want to know.

Today, I feel like I've been acting for most of my adult life. I've known for a couple of years I had a good story to tell but things have crashed so badly recently that I realised I needed to get on and tell it, before it was too late.

The root of my problems began when I started hanging out with a much richer crowd in my hometown of Chigwell, in Essex. By the time I was 19 or 20, I'd decided I would make as much money as one of our most successful family friends – Alan Sugar. I'd make so much bleedin' money that everyone would want to know me. At least that's what I thought. Unfortunately, I ended up becoming famous in the underworld for all the wrong reasons and that's the sort of fame *no one* wants.

It could all have been so different. When I was 12, I decided to set up a business washing Rolls-Royces for all our rich neighbours, and the richest one of all – Alan Sugar – encouraged me in his typical brash way. I was, in a sense, his apprentice. I called myself a 'Rolls-Royce specialist cleaner', and he let me wash his Roller first and then gave me some very handy tips which I have never forgotten. I had no right to say I was a specialist at all, but I acted it out and got away with it. I wish I hadn't, because then I might not have thought I could get away with so much other stuff later in life.

I often try to think to myself, 'Where did it all begin?' And I suppose it's back in those childhood days when I thought I was this Cheeky Charlie who could do anything I damn well pleased. I am a firm believer in the beginning, middle and end philosophy of life and I know it all began then because I was even overspending my pocket money.

This is the first time I have spoken honestly, openly and

publicly about what has become a living nightmare. Even when I went into rehab to try to escape the criminals who were after me at the time, I wasn't 100 per cent honest.

I've buried so much stuff about what I've done over the past 20 years because I was so fucking embarrassed by it all and how I'd got here. There is no defence for it. Why did I do it? It is very hard to talk about because it makes me realise what a fool I've been. I am not hiding anything here but stuff just pops into my head and then it makes me realise things are even worse than I thought.

I often go out to eat with gangsters because it's a good way of softening the blow about not being able to pay my debts to them. And they never have their backs to the door in any public place. I know it's an old cliché, but it's true. Before my troubles started, I used to always face the entrance of any restaurant or bar because I liked people to see me when they came in. But now I do the complete opposite because they might not recognise me so quickly if I have my back to them. I prefer to have a little, sneaky look over my shoulder or I pick a place where I can see in a mirror or reflection who is walking in. That gives me the upper hand. I want to avoid the violence that now so often overshadows my life.

It could all have been so different if I'd never fallen into the 'trap' that has destroyed so many people in money-mad Britain over the past ten years. I thought I could spend what I liked by borrowing money from banks and using credit cards. And when that crashed, I still presumed there'd always be someone around the corner who'd bail me out and then I could just slide back into my normal, safe, middle-class existence with my beautiful wife and two young children.

Anyway, here is my story. I reckon it proves that anyone at any time can end up with a death sentence hanging over them, even if they have never actually committed a crime or laid a finger on anyone else in their entire life.

But then money really is the root of all evil.

Jason Shifrin, 2011

PROLOGUE – PART I
CHIGWELL, ESSEX, FEBRUARY 1983

I'd known Alan Sugar virtually all my life but I'd always been a bit scared of him, in that healthy sort of way you look up to strong adults when you are a kid. I'd been to his huge house round the corner loads of times because I was best friends with his son Simon. I'd seen Alan happy; I'd seen Alan angry; I'd even seen Alan cooking up a storm in the kitchen with a pinny on.

But this time I was facing a different sort of Alan Sugar from the family man I was used to. This was Alan Sugar, the astute businessman, the man who has made a fortune out of being tough and resilient. Now he was about to apprentice me in the fine art of … cleaning Rolls-Royces. I was all ears because I wanted to be just as big a success as he already was back then, even before TV stardom had beckoned.

You see I'd persuaded Alan to let me wash his Rolls-Royce so I could get the hang of it because I'd decided to launch my first ever business as a professional Rolls-Royce cleaner and there were loads of Rollers in Chigwell, I can tell you. I was just 13 years old at the time.

Alan was delighted to be my first customer, mainly because I offered to clean his dark-blue Rolls-Royce Spirit for free. I knew only too well that, once he recommended me to his mates, I'd be coining in the cash and, at £15 a car, that would turn out to be bloody good money for a schoolboy.

It was a Sunday morning and Alan had expertly reversed the Spirit out of the double garage of his detached mansion with its long driveway before barking at me in that inimitable way of his, 'Right, son. Off you go. I expect it to be bloody spotless by the time I get back in an hour.'

Seconds later, he'd jumped in his wife Ann's Jag. She was driving and they went off to play tennis. It's funny to think back to it now but I suppose my Sunday-job aspirations definitely made me one of Alan Sugar's youngest apprentices. He didn't exactly give me any advice, but then that's not Alan's way, even when he's glaring at all those hopefuls on his TV show. But I already knew him well enough back then to realise it was always sink or swim with Alan. He was a tough, uncompromising character but he always seemed to have a soft heart underneath it all and he most definitely respected anyone who had the bottle to start up a business on their own.

After Alan and Ann had disappeared round the corner in the Jag, I got stuck into cleaning that Roller with incredible precision and quickly found myself sweating buckets, even though it was mid-February and I was breathing steam in the frosty morning air. I was well aware that the great Alan Sugar would give me hell if I didn't do a good job and I wanted to prove to him that I was trustworthy and capable of running my own business, even though I hadn't even taken my O-levels yet. But then I'd already recognised Alan's unique talents, the same skills that millions now watch on *The Apprentice*. I worshipped the ground he walked on to a great extent and I wanted to be him. I wanted to mirror his success and make my own family immensely proud in the process.

By the time I spotted Ann Sugar's Jag waiting for their electronic gates to open before they swept in, I was on the last hurdle of cleaning that Rolls. I'd promised myself I'd have it immaculate by the time he got back.

The Jag purred in through the gates and headed up the driveway towards the Roller. I took a big gulp and tried to act cool by keeping my head down and not even noticing them approaching. I bent down and continued polishing carefully at the front bumper chrome.

Seconds later, I heard Alan's footsteps on the drive. I looked up as if I'd only just realised he'd arrived home. But I could see from the expression on his grizzly five o'clock shadow face that he knew I was playing games.

'So … you call yourself an expert car cleaner, do you?'

I nodded nervously and tried to look him straight in the eye because I remembered how he'd said to his son Simon that you should always look people in the eye when you are doing business with them.

Just then, Alan opened the driver's door of the Rolls and stopped in his tracks. 'What d'you call this, then?'

I didn't know what he was on about so I said nothing. I knew I'd cleaned all the car doors and the windows really carefully and believed there was no way he could have spotted a scrap of dirt.

'Come 'ere, son,' he said, beckoning me over in his direction with his forefinger.

I walked nervously round the front of the Roller towards him.

'See this?' he said, now stabbing his finger downwards. 'That's the frame of the door and it's not been cleaned.'

I swallowed really hard then and looked down and he was right. I just hadn't thought about that bit under the door.

'Well?' he said gruffly.

'I'm sorry, Alan. I didn't realise …'

'Didn't realise? If you wanna be my apprentice, son, you'd better learn fast.'

I never forgot those words because of his later TV stardom. And it has taken more than 25 years for me to realise that Alan Sugar's words of encouragement – while well intentioned – made me seek out a career in the world of business which unfortunately turned into a disaster.

And only time will tell if I can salvage anything from Alan Sugar's well-intentioned advice all those years ago.

PROLOGUE – PART II

BOCA RATON, FLORIDA, JANUARY 2004

It was 20 years later and I was once again preparing myself to face Alan Sugar, but this time under very different circumstances. I was heavily in debt and needed a very big loan and I knew in my heart of hearts he would never bail me out. Why should he?

The night before that meeting was scheduled, I walked out on to the hotel balcony where I had been staying with my family to try to escape the reality of what was going on in my life. I was sweating buckets after five hours without a wink of sleep. I'd gone out there originally to clear my head but then I started thinking about jumping.

I stood there for ages. Surely the logical thing to do was to jump? It had to be easier than crawling to Alan Sugar for a loan I knew he wouldn't give me. It also had to be easier than facing the killers awaiting me back in the UK. I had gangsters and money-lenders calling me every minute of the day and night, threatening to murder me because of the money I owed them. I was in the biggest hole in the entire world and I could only see one way out.

I looked down at the swimming pool 18 floors below my hotel suite. The bright Florida lights sparkled in the distance. It was nearly time to go.

Earlier that evening, I'd been in the room with my wife Nicole and our one-year-old, Jacob, and Arabella, who was three. They were so innocent and unaware of what was happening. We just seemed like a normal family on holiday then. We'd been away in Florida for two weeks but it wasn't until the second week that I started to explain to my wife that I had these 'problems'. And these 'problems' consisted of millions of pounds of debts and threats to kill me if I did not pay them back from a group of sinister characters who looked as if they had walked off the set of *The Sopranos*.

It wasn't until we'd put the kids to bed a few hours earlier that I completely opened up to Nicole, though. She had such a pained look on her face as I told her the full extent of what was happening. Now she knew that we really were in deep trouble and no one was likely to bail us out.

So, now, to stop the pain I was causing to my loved ones, I was going to jump off that balcony. That would solve everything and then they could get on with their lives without me dragging them any further down. I had heaped enough shame on them. Now it was time to leave them all in peace.

My wife hadn't noticed me walking out there in the middle of the night because she'd finally fallen asleep after a lot of tears. Even after telling her what was happening, I'd still felt optimistic. But that was always my problem – I couldn't see the shit until it had hit the fan.

My wife could be very pessimistic at times and she always pinned all her hopes on others when there was a problem. That meant I was the one who usually came to the rescue, but not this time. She always phoned me whenever there was the slightest problem, but that had stopped me sharing my problems with her until now.

Earlier, I'd lain in bed for four or five hours just thinking and thinking about what I could do to stop those evil characters coming after me to repay millions of pounds I simply didn't have.

The next morning, I was supposed to go and see Alan Sugar at his house near the hotel to plead for his help. I was due to meet Alan at 9.00am and then at 12.30pm I was scheduled to fly back with my family to the UK. Everything rested on that one meeting, but, in reality, I knew he was highly unlikely to help me. Why would he? Typically, I'd given my wife some classic Jason 'happy spin' and had made out that everything would be all right because Alan Sugar would rescue me. It was a load of bollocks but at least it meant she could get some sleep under the impression that we would all be OK.

Now I was out on that balcony convinced that I had to end it all. I looked down again at the swimming pool below and decided to aim for that. It didn't seem so bad to jump on to water rather than concrete. And, as I gazed at the glassy surface below,

I started thinking about all the fun I'd had with my kids just a few hours earlier in that same pool. They had been blissfully unaware of what was happening in my life.

I just kept flashing back to being with them all earlier in the day. I remembered holding my daughter as she tried to swim and saying to her, 'Remember this moment.' Why did I say that? Maybe I already knew that I was about to die. I remembered I just kept saying, 'This is the last but one day of our holiday so remember this moment.'

Facing Alan Sugar later that morning would be daunting. I knew he might be quite harsh with me. I wondered if he'd put up that famous Alan Sugar 'wall' because he rarely showed his sentimental side. And I kept coming back to the same thing – why would he bother helping me? It was a waste of time. With Alan Sugar, you either took it or you walked away. That's what they all used to say.

I could see it now. I'd sit there with Alan – my so-called saviour – while he looked at me as if I was some sort of idiot. I was nothing more than a broken man, begging him pathetically for his help when he owed me nothing. This whole thing was going to be a disaster. I was nervous and scared and, worse still, I knew Alan was well aware of why I was going to meet him. I was in the biggest hole you could imagine and I wanted him to haul me out of it.

Why, then, was I even trying to appeal to Alan's generosity? The alternative was flying back to England and facing the music … and possibly the end of my life. It really was as simple as that.

I was facing millions of pounds' worth of debt owed to people who might kill me if I didn't pay them very soon. Yet I simply did not have the money to pay them. These people were set to eat me alive. They'd torture me and then kill me. I was a goner.

So all these thoughts were going round and round my head as I stood there on the edge of that balcony. And, for the first time in my life, I realised why people killed themselves. It was a chilling realisation because it *made sense*.

I'd already been there for 20 minutes, looking down at the wonderfully lit pool and all those sparkling lights in the distance. I felt this surge of clarity go through my head. I could see into the future and I knew that this was the right way to go. Everyone would be rid of me. They wouldn't have to stress about me any longer. Surely I was doing them all a favour? It seemed best to turn this sort of stuff around because that made it all easier to accept.

Then, suddenly, out of the darkness I heard my son crying out for me. I looked down at the pool hundreds of feet below and, for a few seconds, tried to imagine myself leaping towards it. But that image was short-lived because my son called out again.

'Daddy …'

'*Daddy …*'

Hearing him cry out knocked some sense into me. How could I seriously contemplate leaving them for ever? What the hell was I doing? They need me. So, in a sense, my son saved me, although he will never realise this. I suppose I was in a trance that night in Florida. I'd been justifying it all by thinking that my kids would be better off without me. I thought the world would be a better place without Jason Shifrin in it.

'*Daddy ...*'

I turned round and went straight back into the room and tended to my son. He was sitting up in bed saying he was thirsty. I got him a drink and held the glass for him, tipping it very gently, grateful that I was still there to witness such a touching sight.

He seemed worried about me and I found that incredibly moving. It was almost as if he knew I was troubled and he wanted to give me some measure of reassurance. In some ways, he was the adult and I was the child. I could see the concern in his eyes. He was looking into me and it made me feel more secure and relieved that I was there and not lying dead 18 storeys below.

I stayed with him until he fell asleep.

Then I went back to the bedroom. The French doors on to the balcony were still open but I had no interest in going out there again. That awful moment had passed, thank God. I had decided it was all going to be all right, so I calmed down.

I looked at my wife fast asleep and wondered how I could ever have contemplated breaking their hearts and destroying the rest of their lives through such a selfish act. I stepped back in a sense and, for the first time, I truly realised that their existence in my life was all that mattered.

I slipped quietly into bed without disturbing my wife and then I fell asleep.

Until very recently, I never believed in the stars and the spirits, but, when I look back on how things evolved that warm evening in Boca Raton, I wonder if perhaps there was a 'higher being' watching over myself and my family.

My son had definitely sensed something that night in Florida. He 'saved' me. I think he knew what was happening and that's why he called out my name as I stood there contemplating ending my life. That boy knew.

So I'd resisted the temptation to take the coward's way out and now I was back with my family. But that didn't mean the bad people would all go away and leave me alone. They'd still be waiting for me back in London. I would have to face the music. There was no choice for me; they would keep pushing. There was a sense of the inevitable about it all.

So this is where I am. Living on borrowed time.

1

A CHARMED LIFE

There aren't many people who can say they remember their own birth, but I can, because my dad filmed it all. Well, not the gory bits, but a lot of stuff just before and just after I popped out. I was actually born in our modest little house in Wanstead, east London, on 29 March 1970. Back in those days, it was pretty unusual to film everything like that but my dad was mad keen on movies.

I was born at home because my mum hated hospitals. My birth is all on camera from when the cord was cut, although you can't hear any of it because it had no sound.

My dad would have liked to have filmed the actual birth but my mum told him to turn it off or she would kill him. He stopped recording and then started again secretly just as they were cutting the cord. That was typical of my dad – always playful.

I was the ugliest little baby in the world with a lot of dark hair and a squashed-up face so not much has changed in that department. I was about 8lb and I was all creased and weird looking. You can even see the maternity nurse, a big, black lady, attending to the birth, and my older sister is there fast asleep throughout it all. Typical.

My dad filmed it all on 8mm stock and we had to watch it on a projector so it was always a special occasion when he screened it, which made my birth seem even more memorable.

The next bit of the film of my early life shows me in the bed with my mum and sister, who is prodding me with fascination. It was the morning after my birth. I was only just a few hours old but my mum was playing up to the camera by this time. I think she was gloating about being a mum for the second time.

The next bit of my dad's filming shows me still as a baby in a swinging chair and my sister watching me doing stuff. Then there is a pram with an 'L' plate as my mum pushes me up the road. My dad was great – he gave us a lot of loving care and attention and still does to this day. These are happy snapshots of my childhood that help me understand who I am more than most people ever get the chance to. You see, I come from a good, honest, hard-working family. My childhood was idyllic.

My dad bought the camera because he wanted to have something he could keep as a record of our lives. Things were changing fast then. He had a Bang & Olufsen eight-track music system before most people. I think he missed out on big chunks of his own childhood and maybe that's why he was so obsessed with recording his own family on film.

My sister went to Wanstead Jewish Day School and I went to the nearby nursery but I insisted I wanted to go to school with my sister and refused to be dragged into the nursery, so they let me join my sister at that school from a ridiculously young age. Typical of me to nag and nag until I got my own way, I am afraid.

My first proper childhood memory was when I was three or four years old and I had nightmares about *Doctor Who*. I used to find it very scary. I remember calling for my dad and he would come and tuck me in and tell me not to worry about it. Every time I hear the *Doctor Who* music, even these days, it sends a shiver up my spine.

Dad said it was only a TV programme. 'It's not real,' he'd insist. But maybe that was one of my problems in life. I didn't always know where that line was between fact and fiction, reality and fantasy. I suppose I am far too optimistic about everything, which makes me very unrealistic about stuff. So, when I sit down with somebody and they say they need a million pounds, I don't bat an eyelid.

As I got deeper and deeper into trouble in later life, I convinced myself there were all these saviours just around the corner who would never let me get into serious trouble. They'd rescue me. It all goes back to my childhood, I guess.

But my father's home-movie footage proves to me that I had a very good start in life. My parents were always together, and my mum was once described as a 'Full Monty Mum' because she combines being a friend and a brilliant cook with someone who only ever sees the good in her own children. And, trust me, you could not wish to meet a more loyal and loving person.

My grandparents were also around a lot of the time. There was never any violence in my house; I only really remember my dad smacking me once – and I thoroughly deserved it. I was about nine and I was at this primary school, and I had a tutor who insisted my parents take me out of my beloved state school and send me to this horrible private school. I was very miserable and loathed it with a passion. One day, my dad slapped me round the face when I was whining about it all and I crashed into my Scalextric set as I fell on to the floor.

I'd earlier put on a whole performance about not going to my latest school. I built it up and up and basically I pushed my dad into hitting me. It was a slap, not a punch. It didn't even hurt, and he stormed out of the room and went to work, but he didn't linger on it and we put it all behind us very quickly. That's the real sign of a loving family.

Another time, my mum dropped me off at the same private school and I was very upset, so she waited in the car for a bit to make sure I was OK. I ended up running back out of the school gate and jumping straight back in her car and begged her to take me home. I never set foot in that school ever again.

The reason I tell this story is because it was a classic example of when I got my own way and that wasn't such a good thing for my development as a human being. I'd already begun to believe I could get away with anything. My mum doting on me for all the right reasons, however, didn't exactly help, either. She never punished me. She unintentionally gave me this licence to get away with stuff, which may have caused a lot of problems in later life.

My parents had first met when my mum was 16 and my dad was 19. Both of them had left school at 15 and my dad got an apprenticeship in Hatton Garden and became an engraver. He was made redundant when my mum was pregnant with me. That's when he got a shed and opened his own company making jewellery. Being made redundant was the best thing that ever happened to him.

My dad had been one of the only Jews in his school and had had quite a hard time and was picked on a lot. He is a very deep man but I have only ever seen him cry once. He doesn't show all his cards often. He brushes off the past. He is such a reasonable person he'd even make conversation with Adolf Hitler.

When he was younger, he did a lot of work for a little jewellery shop in Gants Hill, Essex, and on one occasion the notorious gangster Charlie Kray came in. My dad didn't have a clue who he was at first and Charlie Kray knew the boss of this place where he worked. Maybe he was casing the joint. Who knows?

Anyway, my dad later recalled that Charlie Kray had a definite presence when he walked into the shop. My dad even asked Kray to get out of the way because he was standing too close to the merchandise. Charlie complied without taking any offence, and it was only afterwards that my dad found out who he was. It's a typical story about my dad because he is a normal, straight-talking kind of guy who never tries to impress people, whoever they are.

My dad was always very calm if there were ever any problems at home. His original job as an apprentice engraver had been highly skilled and it seemed to make him incredibly patient. If you had a trophy, he would engrave it. He never even used instructions to put a toy model together for us. He'd just do it himself.

My dad could even listen to a piece of music on the television or radio and work out how to play it virtually note for note. I am not musical at all, but we do have a cousin who played on one single with Mary Wilson in the Eighties.

So, having been made redundant from the company in Gants Hill, my dad set up business in that shed at the bottom of the garden of our little house. It became his factory and he was soon manufacturing crosses and Stars of David and selling them to wholesalers and they'd usually end up in markets. He was much happier working for himself.

My dad rapidly grew out of that shed and moved to a small factory in Romford. He eventually employed ten people and then went from that factory to a 5,000 sq ft site and his main customers became the vast, nationwide jewellery chain Ratners.

Meanwhile, back at home, other stuff on Dad's home movies included loads of us in the paddling pool and in the garden. I remember we had a Wendy house and I was caught in it one time with a neighbour called Ellie 'mucking around'. I was five or six at the time so it was a big deal and my mum walked in and said, 'Oh my God, what are you doing?' It was typical of me just to smile and try to hope that would help get me out of a mess, which, of course, it always did.

I was six when we moved from our small family home in Wanstead Park Road to 30 Courtland Drive in Chigwell. That was a big step up. That day we moved, I was picked up from school and taken to our new home. I remember it was snowing. The new house had a huge garden that seemed like a park it was so big and the first thing I did was build a snowman.

My grandfather Zida often came round with sweets and money for us and he always believed that all kids had two birthdays every year. When it was my mum's birthday, he'd always buy her brother and sister presents as well. He adored me, and whenever he popped over I'd clean his car and he'd take us to the park.

From an early age, I earned a few bob in the local markets by helping out my granddad. I loved the markets and, in some ways, I regret not going into them full-time later in life. We usually went to the ones at Roman Road and Bermondsey. I'd get up at the crack of dawn but I was never allowed to skip school. Sometimes I earned as much as £5 a day. We'd often get to Bermondsey when it was still dark.

Zida was very Jewish in a lot of ways, even though he was not a practising Jew, and he certainly never tried to hide his Jewishness. If anyone called him a 'yid' in the market, he'd be up for an instant fight. But he never went to a synagogue. He was the most unorthodox of us all in many ways because his religion was his family.

We'd usually go to the markets in my grandfather's tiny Fiat van. Granddad never broke the speed limit and was proud of that but sometimes used to get terrible road-rage and go bananas with other motorists. He also had no sense of direction, unless he knew exactly where he was going. And if my grandfather had to be somewhere, he'd always be hours early for everything.

I loved it at those markets and would be the first one screaming at the top of my voice, 'Handbags a pound … any handbag you want … a pound.' I really got into it.

There were so many people who knew and adored my granddad. In fact, he sold all his handbags for a pound. They were the cheapest handbags in the market. He'd pay 60p or 70p for them and so the mark-up wasn't much.

I worked out he had it all wrong because he wasn't making enough money on each bag. He said he relied on turnover. But with my granddad it was always his way and no other. He'd forever be saying, 'Don't ever owe money … don't get into debt …' and stuff like that. He said you should also always be a truthful person and I'm glad he didn't live to see what happened to me in later life.

So working in the markets helped me pick up a feel for people – who was trouble and who was not. Every single type of person goes to a market and what I liked about it was that you came across them all. The market taught me to size people up quickly. It gave me a sense of instinct. I learned to know when someone was angry with me. I could walk along a street and sense if there was trouble. That meant I was usually two steps ahead of most people.

Both markets were on the edge of notorious council estates,

which meant you got all types there. You'd be told to keep your eyes open for potential thieves and muggers all the time. There was banter among the stallholders and, as a kid, I picked up on it. We were called the 'gay boys' because we were selling handbags. It was a right laugh.

But I never picked up any violent instincts, either through the markets or from school. I only had one fight at school and I felt awful afterwards. It was more like a scuffle than a fight. I beat myself up more for doing it than I did the other kid. I also wasn't one of these kids who got involved in crime when I was young. I wasn't interested in alcohol either. I was always in control of myself and I was more concerned with threats from other people.

My granddad always wore a light-coloured suit and tie, and a trilby hat at the markets and even when he came round on a Saturday. He was very traditional. He never looked at another woman and he adored my Booba, as we always called my granny, although he was quite selfish because he expected her to do everything for him. It's very different today with men.

I suppose I was his favourite grandchild but, in truth, he spoiled all of us. However, I was the only one who phoned him every day. I loved being around him and I'd talk to him about everything. In fact, I was so superstitious that, if I didn't ring him every day, I would worry that something bad might happen to him. Granddad ended up working for my dad into his eighties. However, he smoked 40 cigarettes a day and eventually got so ill he had to have a colostomy bag after contracting bowel cancer. I was there for him whenever he needed me, along with my mum and the rest of the family.

So we were now living in that big house in Chigwell and my dad was driving a very modest, white Fiat 127. Then he bought his first brand-new car – a navy-blue, automatic Rover 3500. We had this sweeping drive and the Rover often slightly blocked it. One day, all the doors of the Rover were unlocked, so I got in the car and decided to pretend to drive it to Southend.

I put the Rover into reverse but my dad hadn't put the handbrake on so it started moving backwards on this big slope. Shit, I thought, but, instead of rectifying it, I simply jumped out of the Rover and the door ended up being bent backwards as it knocked down a garden wall before hitting the Fiat and then rolling right down the drive and out towards the street. Thank God it didn't knock anyone over.

But it did cause a hell of a lot of damage. However, when my mum and dad came rushing out, all they said was: 'Are you OK?' That was it. It was all my fault but I'd got away with it – again! They never bollocked me and my dad blamed himself for not putting the handbrake on. All that mattered to them was that I'd escaped without a scratch on me. It was very nice of them but, in retrospect, I'm not so sure they should have allowed me to get off scot-free.

There is loads of home-movie footage of us in swimming pools on holidays all over the place. We used to go on two or three holidays every year as my dad's business became more and more successful. At Christmas, we'd go to the Hotel Fontainbleau in Miami where the so-called 'Jewish pack' from Essex would often go. Summers when I was a kid usually meant a Mediterranean holiday.

Our family was a closely knit unit and we would often meet friends on holiday. We rarely went away with other groups but we would meet up with them when we were there. Loads of the Jewish pack would be on the same plane as us on the way to Florida at Christmas time. I adored landing at Miami Airport, the hamburgers and the general buzz of being in the States.

Once, my dad met up with some business associates and we all went up in a private plane, which was really scary because it was a tiny little plane and there was a storm. It's one of those childhood experiences I will never forget because, for the first time in my life, I actually thought I was going to die.

Another time on the way from London to Florida with BA, we were caught in a lightning strike and my dad recorded everything on his new mini-cassette recorder. He knew we weren't going to crash and just kept it on. You can hear the fear in all the passengers' voices. It was typical of my dad to record the whole thing.

My friend Jonathan and I often used to go up and down in the Fontainbleau hotel elevator in Florida all afternoon together. We'd pretend our dads owned the hotel and hoped that someone would hear us. The swimming pool seemed like Disneyworld to us kids because it had huge slides and water tunnels.

Years later, my wife and I missed our plane once in Florida and I couldn't resist returning to the Fontainbleau, so we checked in and then straight out again because it was awful. I had all these wonderful memories in my head but the reality was very different. I wanted it to be how I remembered it and, while it was still a perfectly acceptable hotel, the idyllic images of my childhood were so much better than the present-day reality.

2

THE MONEY ROLLS IN

My dad's jewellery-manufacturing business was doing so well that, eventually, in 1982, he was able to afford his first Rolls-Royce. Mind you, I nagged him and nagged him. My granddad always wanted one but he couldn't afford it, so in a way I wanted us to get one for him. I drove Dad nuts looking them up in the *Sunday Times* classified section every weekend and kept pointing them out to him.

Eventually, we found a five-year-old, chocolate-brown Silver Shadow II Rolls-Royce in Southend and set off down to the seaside to pick it up. I was so excited. It had a cream vinyl roof and we even put white wall tyres on it. I think Dad paid about £15,000.

I remember the day we collected that Roller so clearly. My grandfather was already in Southend because it was a hot, sunny day so we went and picked him up in it. Zida virtually flew down the hill to join us when he saw us drive up to meet him. He said afterwards he felt like the king of England in that car. I loved seeing that happy look on his face. He was so proud.

I also remember the cream upholstery and how the middle part of the seats were brown with dark piping and the smell of the leather. There was a vanity mirror with the wood around it and the light fitting with the glass that went over it. It even had an outside temperature gauge in addition to all the regular features. It seemed to float down the road that afternoon.

Mind you, my sister was so embarrassed she wanted to get out, but I was leaning out of the window just screaming with delight, 'Look at us … Look at us!'

I loved being picked up from school in the Roller. But my dad wasn't the flash type so he only brought it out very rarely. I waxed it and cleaned it constantly, although it sat in the garage at home for weeks on end. Once, I sneaked a quick drive in and out of the garage when I was cleaning it but I didn't have the courage to take it any further – yet.

Later, when I was 15, I nicked it and took it out for a proper spin. My mum and dad were away, so me and a friend called Lloyd drove it to Southend. We got pulled over by the police but all they did was ask me to do up my seatbelt. They didn't even ask my age or whether I had a licence. My mate Lloyd was shitting himself but I stayed cool and we got away with it. Not good.

My dad never liked us talking about how much money we had. I wasn't even allowed to tell people that my dad had a jewellery factory for 'security reasons'. I remember he went ballistic when I told some builders in the street what he did for a living.

My mum and dad just weren't flash types. I was flashier than them and I begged them to take me to school in the Roller but I reluctantly understood why they wouldn't.

A teacher at school knew where I lived and had a right chip on his shoulder about me living in a big house. He'd always be telling my class how you could play football in our garden because it was so big. Looking back, that was a really stupid thing to say. I reckon he was jealous.

Quite a few of my school friends' dads were gangsters, though. It sort of came with the territory in Essex. I didn't know it at the time, but found out afterwards. One of my mates' dads – who I think was the uncle of a well-known boxer – had a boxing ring in his house. The dad and the son would get into the ring together and knock the shit out of each other, which was a bit weird.

When I called my friend, I had to ask for 'Dan Boy' because he had the same name as his father. At 13, Dan Boy could beat up much older kids and he was very muscular. He used to look after me a bit like a bodyguard. But I tended not to get too heavily involved with my school friends outside of school.

Following that incident with my dad's Rover, I got a definite taste for cars and one day I was round at my friend Simon Sugar's house. They had this tiny bubble car for the gardener on their huge estate near us in Chigwell. Simon and I often used to drive the bubble car around. It only had 60 miles on the clock and most of that was from us driving it around. It was like a mini-sized car and we burned the clutch out after a couple of crazy driving sessions round the lawn.

Overall, I wasn't really naughty at school. I was cheeky but not a troublemaker. I tried to be friendly with all the teachers, although generally I found school a bit pointless as I knew full well what I wanted to do – make money. I didn't need school to tell me that. I was a bright kid, alert and always on the lookout for an opportunity. What more did I need? I even got one of my old teachers a job working at my dad's jewellery factory.

I was forced much against my will to do sports at school and I was useless at it all. I would often be stuck in goal for football and I remember I once saved a ball but no one congratulated me. They just gave the other bloke a lot of stick for not getting the ball in the net.

But one thing I never got away with was fighting with my sister. I hit her over the head with a pole in the garden once. But I never did it again after that incident because my parents went absolutely mad at me. Mind you, I was always trying to wind my sister up. I would hide her clothes to annoy her. I still wind her up to this day. I would take the mickey out of her friends when they called up. She didn't take it very well.

Despite my dad being great in so many ways, he did do some things that really grated with me. He was always looking at the price of dishes on the menu when we were in restaurants. He was addicted to asking for a discount on everything and shopping was not a pleasant experience with him because he was always trying to stop us spending money. In hindsight, this definitely had an opposite effect on me because it made me even more carefree with money. I wanted to be able to have whatever I wanted. So it's certainly true to say my dad sent me the other way. I wanted to spend, spend, spend all the time. When I went out with Simon and Alan Sugar, we'd always go to the posh local Chinese and no one ever seemed to care about how much it all cost.

Even when it came to my dad's car, he was careful not to spend too much and was obsessed with having it serviced only when he really had to. Then he'd drum into me to only spend what I had and not what I didn't have. Credit cards were only used sparingly and he paid them off at the end of every month really carefully. It all seemed a bit boring to me.

We never flew Club class on aeroplanes when we were growing up. All of our close friends would appear to be above us in terms of wealth; I felt a bit inferior to them and it was very soul-destroying to get on an aeroplane to go on holiday with these friends and they'd turn left to Club and we'd turn right to economy. In hindsight, how many of them were just keeping up with the Joneses, which my dad was never interested in? He just paid what he could afford, and how I wish now that that lesson had rubbed off on me.

Sure, my mum and dad spoiled me by giving me nice toys and presents for my birthdays but some of my richer friends always seemed to have a way of belittling me by getting something much better for their celebrations.

Typically, my father even put a coin-box telephone in each of our bedrooms so my sister and I had to pay for our own calls. But that didn't stop me. I just unplugged it and used another phone. The trouble is that, although I thought it was pathetic at the time, I now realise that he was trying to teach me the value of money. He had my interests at heart. I just didn't appreciate that.

From an early age, I took a great interest in share prices in the paper. Shares in Amstrad – owned by Alan Sugar – had just gone public and I was intrigued by it all. So I started buying shares myself with the money I earned from various jobs at home. I spent more than £1,000 on shares when I was still at school.

Around this time, my parents did splash out on a flat in Spain next to the bullring in Marbella, just above the notorious marina of Puerto Banus, right in the heart of the Costa del Crime. My dad even allowed me to drive our hire car in nearby fields.

My dad was still doing well and he'd got into the imitation-diamond market; he was one of the first people to manufacture them and I remember well-known jeweller Gerald Ratner driving my dad mad because he wanted so much of the product for his stores. That's when he made big money. The flat in Spain was a result of that success.

I soon had a group of friends, many of whose families all had flats in Spain, and we often used to go there at the same time. I remember as a kid walking round Puerto Banus and looking in Sinatra's bar, where all the criminals in their gold jewellery hung out; I knew they were bad people, just by the look of them, even though my dad would always be trying to look the other way.

I was also very aware of expensive watches like Rolexes from a very early age. I would hear my parents' friends going on about them all the time. Our family friend Cyril Dennis would wear the 'JR' from *Dallas* gold number. A lot of my parents' friends seemed to be influenced by TV programmes like *Dallas* and *Dynasty* – shoulder pads, big hair and all that jewellery. I remember begging my mum and dad to let me buy a fake Rolex but they would never let me. They thought it was naff for a kid to be wearing such an expensive-looking watch. But I wanted to feel important; I didn't care what other people thought.

To me, a Rolex was a bit like a Rolls-Royce. I wanted to buy my own Rolex but I was gutted because I didn't have nearly enough money. It was a status symbol. Having a good watch became an obsession to me.

Mind you, I loved all watches. Often, I'd be at my grandparents' if my parents were working and my granddad would let me sift through a big bag of old watches he had and I'd mend some of them and get them going again. I would wear different watches when I went out. Most kids only had one. My mum and dad bought me a Disney Mickey Mouse watch with a Mickey Mouse who ticked, and I spent months trying to repair it when it went wrong and I made it work in the end. I loved taking them apart and rebuilding them. It made me feel responsible. It was such a brilliant feeling when I got one of them repaired and it worked.

I also had toy model Rolls-Royces in my bedroom plus a huge picture of one on my wall. I even had a T-shirt with the Rolls-

Royce symbol. If I ever spotted a Rolls-Royce in a car park, I'd go and have a good look at it.

I was never given money at home – I had to earn it. It was after doing the markets with my granddad that I set myself up as a 'Rolls-Royce Car Cleaning Specialist'. I printed up leaflets with my phone number and dropped them all around Chigwell because there were loads of Rolls-Royces in the area.

The Rolls-Royce cleaning business had been inspired by how difficult it was to clean my dad's Roller, especially the white wall tyres. The only way to clean them was with a Brillo pad but most people did not realise that. I was so serious about it I even had a couple of books about the history of Rolls-Royces at home.

I used the Silvo stuff for the chrome and I had a chamois-leather and special car wax. I set up this business on my own after originally starting it with my friend Jonathan Dennis, but he lasted about a day because he couldn't stand the pressure of humping all the cleaning stuff around, plus I don't think his parents were overly impressed.

As it turned out, Alan Sugar's navy-blue Rolls-Royce Spirit was the first one I cleaned professionally, although I didn't charge him. You could say he was the guinea pig. He let me clean it but then he criticised me afterwards. Alan hardly ever drove it himself as he had a chauffeur and it was very important to him that, when you opened the door, you could see that the frame was as clean as the rest of it. I did it for free because I wanted to clean it and it was an honour for me, in a sense.

Once I'd gone back and cleaned up the frame, Alan came

strutting out and said, 'That's very nice … that's very nice …' and kept walking around it. Then he said, pointing at the door frame, 'You always have to remember that that part is very important.'

He was very impressed overall with my performance. I cleaned his car a few times over that period and he ended up giving me my first Amstrad word processor as a 'fee'.

I suppose you could say I passed my car-cleaning apprenticeship with Alan Sugar. I didn't want cash off him because he was my best friend's dad, but I wasn't going to turn down that free computer. I ended up with about six main clients for the cleaning business, but, as I charged them £15 a car, I made loads of money.

I'd charge my 'clients' £30 for a proper wash 'n' wax. One of them was a local villain, who was well dodgy. He bought a brand-new Rolls-Royce every year. His wife had a Merc and he asked me to clean the wife's Merc for the same price, so he'd pay me once a week to do this for £60, which was big money. I often made as much as £200–£300 a week. Sometimes I'd witness things I'd rather not have seen, like family arguments, but on the whole everyone treated me well.

I had to be very careful not to end up scratching the bodywork. At first, I didn't realise that, if I dropped the chamois-leather on the floor and got a bit of grit stuck to it, then I'd end up scratching the paintwork.

Alan Sugar was the only one who questioned whether I was up to that job of cleaning the Rollers of Chigwell. 'How do you know how to do it then?' he'd ask. 'What makes you qualified? You didn't even clean the inside of the doors the first time.'

So, now, every time I see the inside of the doors of any car I think of Alan Sugar.

I remember later watching the first two years of *The Apprentice* and he was exactly like the Alan Sugar I knew so well – there was no TV-generated front. But now it doesn't seem that he is as natural. He doesn't swear any more, but that is part of who he is, so it's a shame, I think, that the BBC have prevented him from being true to himself.

In many ways, Alan was such a regular type of guy. Most of the time, he was either out on business meetings or in bed. The Sugars had three kids. The first time I ever slept at their huge house, I remember at 5.00am Alan was screaming at his dog trying to catch it after it escaped. There was a rather bizarre atmosphere in the house and Alan's son Simon definitely found it more relaxing staying at my house. The Sugars had a live-in husband and wife who looked after their home. Alan actually did a lot of his own cooking at the weekend. He loved risotto, which he'd present to all of us as if it was the greatest thing in the world.

Back in our less grand Chigwell street, nearly everyone knew me. I was cheerful, happy, hard-working and charming. I loved chatting to people. Cleaning Rolls-Royces let me into these rich people's lives. I got a taste for it and I wanted more.

One guy I cleaned for had an 'A'-reg Spirit and we used to sit at his kitchen table and look up the price of other Rollers in the *Sunday Times*. He took me very seriously and I liked that. I knew exactly what a car was worth back in those days. I used to bank all the money from the cleaning business in the Woolwich Building Society. The main purpose of earning money back then was to get my own car. My dad made it clear he would not buy me one, so I was determined to get one for myself.

3

DIAMOND IN
THE ROUGH

When I was 13, I got a Saturday job in a shop in Kingsland Road in the heart of the old East End. It was a big, double-fronted menswear shop with a second, smaller shop next to it. That job turned into a complete eye-opener and probably made me grow up more than anything else in my childhood. My first shock was discovering that married men had affairs, because up until then I had no idea about that sort of thing.

A lot of women who had husbands in prison would come into the shop and the owner would look after them financially in exchange for sex in the back store room. He obviously used to pretend it wasn't happening but the manager of the shop used to say to me, 'Don't you know what's going on in there?'

Then I used to mutter, 'Jesus!' each time another woman went in the back with the boss. I was completely freaked out at first. I came from a happy family unit where no one even knew what the word adultery meant.

I never thought that married people had affairs. I was very naïve. But when the manager said, 'I promise you … he is shagging those women,' I'd go into that room and there would be spunk hanging off the boxes and he was right. Of course, I knew people got divorced and had sex with other people, but to see this first-hand with a married man was pretty shocking to me. And he was also a neighbour and my dad's age at the time. He had thick, brushed-back, grey hair and was a bit slimy and very Jewish. I used to see him go out the back as he threw me out of the shop, often when the women came in to 'see' him.

One day I was in the main shop with the owner when this aggressive bloke came in and the boss sent me off to the tailor up the road. When I came back later and asked him what was happening, he said it was fine and nothing to concern myself about.

Then, just as we were about to shut up the shop that same night, a car pulled up and four black guys got out and came in and locked the door behind them. Then one of them picked up a letter spike and started threatening us with it. Another one then yelled, 'Give us the fucking money … Give us the fucking money …' over and over. I just stood by the front door pleading desperately for them to let me leave. After all, I was just a kid and I was shitting myself.

But then one of them told me, 'Stay there. You'll be all right.' They weren't threatening me but they knew I would go to the police so they refused to let me go.

Then, suddenly, all these police cars screeched up outside the shop and officers burst in. Moments later, I remember ending up standing behind this big copper because I was so scared. It turned out the owner had pressed a panic button, which had alerted the police, thank God.

The police could clearly see that something was going on but no one was saying a thing. It was farcical in a way. The police got very pissed off and eventually they took the men away for questioning. It turned out it was a protection racket and the police set up cameras and everything around the shop the following Saturday, and, when the same mob came back, 14 armed police raided and arrested them this time with the evidence. I never worked at that shop again, though.

After the owner of the shop drove me home that night, I told my parents everything about that first attack and they were a bit angry with him. He never came in to explain to my parents what had happened and I think there was a dark side to him that we never knew about. It made me decide to get into karate and ju jitsu myself. I wanted to protect myself and not be bullied by people like that.

Alan Sugar's younger son, Daniel, and I joined a local karate club. We even bought ourselves black belts and changed them to white when we got there. On one occasion, we were showing off, doing moves on each other on the train ride to the club, and all of a sudden we noticed two skinheads watching us scowling. They were just about to come into our carriage when we jumped out and made a run for it to avoid them.

That incident with the protection racket at the shop also made me very scared of black people for a long time after that. I was on a flight to Spain on holiday not long afterwards and got completely freaked out by a black guy sitting nearby. I kept trying to convince my dad that he was one of those blokes who had raided the shop for the protection money. It was a stupid over-reaction from a very freaked-out kid.

I became even more observant of people after what happened in the shop. I watched how they behaved and weighed up whether I had a reason to be scared of them. I could tell if people were troublemakers, but not always gangsters; that would come later. My mum had always been very nervy about other people, so I picked up some of those vibes from her. I remember we went on holiday to Paris once and ended up in a hotel room next to a brothel and my mum almost had a heart-attack about it.

At our flat in Marbella, Spain, we'd often be out having dinner somewhere and I'd see a load of blokes in white suits and jewellery and my mum and dad would insist I ignored them all. But, as I learned much later, real criminals don't stand out; it's only the bullies who make a show of themselves.

Most of the people I hung out with in Spain were Jewish from Essex, north London and Manchester. We all went out at night in Spain as kids. It was great because we were allowed out much later than in England. We'd often hang out at the posh hotels and pretend to be more grown up than we really were.

On one holiday in Spain I became romantically involved with

one girl who had a boyfriend and I managed to somehow talk myself out of getting beaten up. That was typical of me. This boy had run up to me and accused me of snogging his girlfriend. I said that wasn't the case, but then I explained to him that I thought she had broken up with him and he accepted it. Once again, I avoided a beating. My charm and acting ability was already virtually on automatic pilot.

I decided I wanted to get into the jewellery trade so, still aged 13, I got a new Saturday job in a jeweller's shop and I also continued cleaning Rolls-Royces. The jeweller's where I worked was a tiny place called Hatton's and every gangster in the area seemed to come in there to get his jewellery. I soon worked out who the important 'faces' were.

I was paid about twenty quid every Saturday. The man who ran the business would buy gold from the customers and they would try to get him involved in all sorts of stuff. He once had to recruit armed guards after falling out with some villains, who were well-known bouncers. One of them later got shot and imprisoned.

These shady characters would often come in the shop with thousands in cash and slap it down for a ring they'd ordered. They'd park their flash cars right outside the shop on a yellow line. None of them seemed to care about stuff like parking tickets. I liked their attitude.

There was this one guy called John who was later linked to a massive drugs factory and now lives in France. His father-in-law was another top gangster and, when he came in once, I was ordered to leave the shop. But, just as I was going, John threw me the keys to his white Porsche 911 Turbo and told me to take it for a ride. I'd just turned 14.

So I drove it nervously down Chigwell High Road. It had a really wide body with a huge aerodynamic wing on the back. I was in heaven, although it was a hard car to drive; I was more used to Dad's Roller. It deserved to be driven round a track, not a normal road. Anyway, I managed to get it back to where it was parked in one piece and then waited patiently by the door to the shop until he came out. He was in there 40 minutes.

What is weird is that many of those characters would come back into my life years later when I least needed them. The seeds came from when I worked in that shop in Chigwell as a kid.

There was another villain with a Corvette Stingray who was always trying to flog rings and stuff in the shop. He clearly thought he was Mr Big and used to intimidate me quite a bit. I ended up living three or four doors away from him in later life and he was one of the three or four people who caused me a lot of problems.

There were many others, including a guy who owned a famous villains' pub. They all had Porsches, Mercs, BMWs and Bentleys. There was never any threat to me but the shop owner would often tell me to get lost when they turned up. He'd say, 'Do me a favour and go up the road and buy some sweets, sandwich and a drink.' The owner was 6ft 2in and a hell of a character. He was a hard worker but I think the characters would always try to talk him into doing dodgy business. He was about ten years older than me. He wasn't a criminal, and he was very good to me, and to this day I still have a lot of time for him.

He always let me know when I should be extra careful, by saying, 'They're fuckin' dangerous people … you don't want to mess around with him. They're complete nutters …' It's a shame I didn't take his advice.

I later saw a huge story in the local paper after the dad of that villain with the Porsche died and they had at least 40 cars at the funeral and it made a big piece. The headline said something like 'LOCAL GANGSTER DIES' and I realised then it was the Porsche guy's father.

More law-abiding customers included Lionel Blair, the dancer, and World Cup winner Sir Geoff Hurst, plus Liam Brady of Arsenal. Hurst lived in my parents' road. We were his local jeweller's shop.

Occasionally, I'd spot the same dodgy characters when I went out with my parents to one particularly well-known local Italian restaurant. As usual, Mum and Dad would try to look the other way, while I was desperately trying to catch their eyes because I was in awe of them to a certain degree. It got me thinking about how they earned all that cash. There was a swagger about them that I really envied.

Back in the shop, those same villains often bunged out huge tips and at Christmas they'd always hand over twenties and fifties. Those people only ever dealt in cash. Credit cards were for straight, 'normal' people and the 'normal' people were much more horrible to deal with. They were a complete pain in the arse; they never paid their bills on time. 'Normal' people were nothing but aggro. The villains knew the score; they never pushed it. They were a pleasure to do business with so long as you didn't cross them.

Meanwhile, my grandfather was still trying to teach me some good habits like not lying to anyone and appreciating the value of money. I hadn't been academic at school and my dad was having a go at me for not working hard enough and then my grandfather would chip in, 'What's one plus one?'

'Two.'

'How many pennies in a pound?'

'One hundred.'

Then he'd turn to my dad and say, 'He's fine,' while giving me an enormous wink.

I remember that so clearly. I regret not working harder at school. I'd sit there and do nothing and then come home every afternoon. I didn't even get to do O-levels, except in drama, which I got a 'B' in, and art. Those were my entire qualifications.

I remember I was halfway through one exam and I looked at my friend Dan Boy and said, 'Have you had enough of this?' and he said, 'Yeah.' And that was the last time I sat an exam at school.

My dad was always engaging virtual strangers in conversations about their jewellery so I guess I picked up that knack of talking to anyone from him. It certainly got me out of some very tight spots.

On one occasion, I was with my mate Lloyd in his Ford Fiesta XR-2 40 when we cut this bloke up in a van and, all of a sudden, four heavies jumped out and came after us. One of them punched Lloyd and all I could see was the word 'LOVE' engraved on this bloke's fist in a tattoo. I begged this guy not to punch me and pleaded with him, 'Please don't hit me … I told my friend not to drive like that.'

And you know what? It worked. I didn't get punched (but they did break the aerial) and it once again convinced me that I could talk my way out of anything. In hindsight, I wish I hadn't got away with it. I should have got a beating and then maybe I wouldn't have got into all this trouble later in life.

Even back then, I always told myself I had money coming in, so why should I worry? From my late teens, I was spending like it was going out of fashion. I'd go on a skiing holiday with my mates and blow a fortune in a week and we weren't even in full-time jobs yet.

The only thing I didn't spend money on was drugs because I couldn't stand them; I don't like being out of control. I also don't like not knowing what my brain is doing. A lot of people in my age group were into weed back then, but I've only tasted it once and it was horrible. I remember when I was 12, my mum gave my sister and me a cigarette and then told us to smoke it in front of her and it put us off tobacco for life. It was a brilliant example of good parenting.

But my mum and dad also had other more obsessive priorities. Under no account was I going to be allowed to marry a non-Jewish girl. They made it very clear, although they were always very welcoming to any girlfriend who came to the house. I guess it's a form of racism at the end of the day, but us Jews won't have it because we say we were persecuted.

Another typical Jewish thing was that I was never allowed out on Friday nights, even though I was a good kid back then and I would hardly have got into any trouble.

But, to be fair, overall, being Jewish was never a real problem growing up. Sure, I was singled out and made aware I was 'the Jew' in some groups, but it wasn't so bad and I knew how to talk my way out of trouble anyway.

So, I left school determined to get a full-time job. Initially, I went into loads of jeweller's shops in the West End but they didn't want a 15-year-old. I even waltzed into the Jack Barclay Rolls-Royce showroom in Mayfair but they laughed me out of there and I certainly wasn't keen on working my way up from being a crap second-hand-car dealer in Essex.

No – watches and jewellery were a much better bet. I met this bloke called Russell who had a mobile-phone shop in Gants Hill and he asked me for a ladies and gents Rolex worth about £8,000 for the pair. I bought them off a trader in Hatton Garden, but then, all of a sudden, Russell cancelled the order and I found out that he'd dealt directly with the same supplier, which was completely out of order. It was the first time I'd been shafted on a deal and it made me see a different side to people. It made me more suspicious.

That disaster sort of made me want a proper, full-time job because it seemed safer. I was eventually hired by a jeweller's shop in Hatton Garden. The first day of work, I walked in with a suit on, even though no one else on the entire staff wore one. Every time someone came in the shop that day, they approached me first because I was wearing a suit. Within a few days, everyone had to wear one.

My dad was already well known in Hatton Garden because he was by now the fifth-largest manufacturer of jewellery in the UK. But I got that job on my own because I deliberately did not use my real name. I just walked in the shop off the street and told them that I had been working part-time in Chigwell. It was the biggest retail premises in Hatton Garden. I knew I'd do well because I am definitely better at selling things that I like. It's one of my weaknesses. I can't actually bullshit in that sense.

Obviously, once I had got the job, I told them my real name. They knew of my dad but not personally, and it felt so good to have got that job on my own merit.

Back home in Chigwell, people like Alan Sugar were well on their way to their first 10 million by this time and I watched his progress with fascination. I wanted a piece of that luxury lifestyle and I didn't care how I went about it.

4

LIVING IT LARGE

Back in the real world, I was on £49 a week in that first job so still had quite a way to go yet. I was told by the owner of the shop in Hatton Garden that I had to learn the trade and stand behind some old dear at the counter. I was supposed to observe and say nothing, but that wasn't my style. I wanted to get involved.

In my first week, this guy came in looking for a strap for his vintage watch. I was polishing a gold watch strap at the time and persuaded him to buy it for £560, instead of the much cheaper leather strap he'd originally wanted. The manager was very pleased.

After that, I was allowed to sell stuff under £1,000 and that first week I also sold a diamond ring. The owner of the shop rewarded me with an extra fiver. I thought that was a joke. He really didn't appreciate me. I soon learned that, if you could make a profit, then just do it. You didn't have to have a huge mark-up. The minimum mark-up was 10 per cent, but it was really all about volume of trade.

Then, on my second week in that Hatton Garden job, I 'earned' a very special different kind of 'bonus'. There was a window display area behind a curtain in the front window and we all used to go in there to get jewellery out. One day, I was in this window display area and the manageress came on to me. She was 30 and I was 15. We ended up bonking behind the window. It was like a schoolboy fantasy come true.

The trouble is I told a couple of mates in the shop what had happened and, within an hour, virtually the whole of Hatton Garden knew about it. She was married, but then she got friendly with some Arabs and used to go out with them, and they bought a lot of expensive stuff in the shop. She ended up running off with one of those Arabs a few months later and we never saw her again.

Not surprisingly, my finances rapidly got in a mess. After obtaining my first credit card, I pushed it to the limit and only paid it off a bit at a time. When my dad saw my bills after they arrived in the post at home, he went ballistic about it. 'How could you not pay your bill?' he'd shout at me. But I didn't care.

Then, after just six months at that first jeweller's, I decided to move on and headed for another shop in Hatton Garden called Eric Ross. I went from £49 a week on that first job to £200 plus commission and overtime on top. Working six days a week, I could earn up to £500 a week, which was big money back then for a 16-year-old.

I had known my new boss Clive for years and he even had a flat near my family in Spain. Clive was openly quite flash and sometimes used to give me a lift in his Rolls-Royce because he lived near us in Chigwell. I even had a bit of a crush on his wife, Andy, who'd also given me a ride home a few times when I was still at school with one of his kids. Noel Gallagher bought that Roller from him a few years later. Naturally, I loved going to and from work in the Roller with Clive.

Clive's kids used to come in the shop regularly during school holidays and they'd piss the staff off no end. On one occasion, the manager got so irritated by Clive's son that he pushed him in a fit of temper. I watched it happen and felt I had no choice but to chin the manager because there was no excuse for a 30-year-old to push a 12-year-old kid to the floor. The manager then got the sack and I took his job, which meant even more money.

But there were a few close shaves; a guy once came into the shop with a Dunhill watch and another member of staff said they weren't interested so I ended up buying it for 50 quid, even though it retailed at about £500–£600. It was a really good deal. I got a right bollocking, even though I felt I had done nothing wrong. Obviously, the shop should have bought the watch and made the profit.

My social life at the time consisted of driving around with my mates going to restaurants, bars and clubs. Most of the time, we kept out of trouble but sometimes it just came looking for us. Occasionally, we'd get chased by people with baseball bats and knives out on the streets of north and east London. My mates always had flashy, boy racer-type cars which seemed to attract no end of trouble. On the way to a concert at Wembley once, we ended up with a snooker ball coming through the back window.

I began to notice that some of the people I encountered at that time really didn't like me and my mates because we were seen as the 'rich boys' from Chigwell. One night, two lorryloads of manure were dropped outside my mate's house. It was a pathetic thing to do but clearly we'd upset a few people, although they didn't have the courage to talk to us directly about it, so I never got to the bottom of it.

I was staying at Simon Sugar's house one Saturday night and my mate Big Paul got lost on the way home and we didn't get back to the Sugars' home until 2.00am. By this time, they had a huge, detached mansion in acres of land with a swimming pool and a tennis court. They also had a hall that seemed as big as a football pitch with an incredibly echoey, black-and-white marble floor.

Alan wife's Ann greeted us at the door and we were told to creep up the stairs to bed quickly before Alan heard us. But then the great man himself appeared at the top of the stairs. 'Where the fuck have you been? We've been worried sick. Bloody idiots.' Then he said to me, 'Pick up the phone in that fuckin' bedroom. Your bloody dad is on the line.'

My dad said not to worry about it and he would speak to me in the morning. He was cringing about it all. Alan's anger soon died away but he could certainly be very scary when he was in a bad mood. Not someone to be crossed. Yet, like any good father, he was simply concerned about his son's wellbeing. You may think I got away with it, but my father was just as worried and my mum would have been climbing the walls.

There were lighter moments with Alan Sugar. He once had to go to a chiropractor, and Simon and I went with him because it was a good excuse to ride in the Roller. We cried with laughter because he was in such pain when the chiropractor started clicking him back into place. Looking back on it, it was especially funny because, for once in his life, Alan Sugar was powerless.

Back at my day job in the Hatton Garden jeweller's, we used to get many strange characters in that shop, including a lot of gypsies. They always turned up in Mercs. They were usually uneducated, really overweight and stank to high heaven, but they often spent as much as £100,000 on jewellery. It was always cash, although it was difficult to understand what they were saying half the time. But the gypsies loved doing deals and we'd make them diamond-encrusted brooches and pins for their little kids and stuff like that. I was entrusted to count their cash after they handed it over. I loved handling the notes. But when you count £100,000 that has been literally kept under a caravan, it does stink to high heaven. I couldn't get the smell off my hands for days but I have to admit there is nothing quite like seeing that much cash to make you want to have more of it yourself. Whenever the film *Snatch* is screened on TV, it always brings back the memories of those days.

I had to check the cash very carefully in case it was fake. Once you start counting money, you can definitely feel the slight difference in a fake note. But, to be fair, the gypsies would always immediately change the fake ones without any argument. They were just trying it on.

My mum and dad were very happy I was working in Hatton Garden. My father wanted me to work for him eventually, but he liked me getting an 'apprenticeship', so to speak. Life seemed good, although I was overspending to a ridiculous degree considering my real salary, but I didn't seem to really care.

Around this time, I also met my future wife Nicole for the first time, through a mutual friend called Lucy. She was 5ft 7in with long, blonde, straight hair and we hit it off immediately. I had met her mum once before because she'd been a customer in the jewellery shop where I'd worked when I was younger. Nicole was the youngest of three daughters and they lived in this huge, gated house near us in Chigwell.

Nicole and I fell for each other instantly. I adored her long hair and model looks and it was no big surprise when we started dating. We'd often go to Rossi's ice-cream shop in Barkingside on a Sunday afternoon and then to Busby's in Tottenham Court Road, which was hired out as a Jewish venue on Sunday nights.

My favourite groups back then were Wham!, Duran Duran and Spandau Ballet. I also loved Luther Vandross and Gloria Estefan. I was earning good money by other young people's standards, at least £500 a week. 'Off duty' I favoured white jeans, pixie boots and I looked a bit like a pop star – or so I thought. In truth, I looked a bit of a wanker. I also had a lot more hair than I have now. It was curly and dark and came down at the back. I used to work all weekends and then I'd have one day off in the week and me and a mate would pick Nicole up from school and take her home.

Then one day about a month after we started dating, some bloke I know said to me, 'Isn't she ugly?' and that ruined the whole relationship for me. I didn't realise he was just jealous of me and I stupidly decided I didn't want to be going out with someone who was considered ugly and so I finished with her. The trouble with Nicole and me at that time was that we were really too young to get serious. It would be another seven years until we were reunited.

The truth is that back then I much preferred going on holidays with the lads rather than girls. We'd all go to Courchevel in the French Alps. Jonathan Dennis broke his leg in three places and had to come home in an air ambulance paid for by his dad.

Eventually, I saved up about £4,000 and I found a Fiesta Dash in the paper. We had this friend whose daughter had a husband with yet another brown Roller. He was a bit of a Rod Stewart-lookalike. This fellow was 24 when he bought his first Rolls-Royce and he took me to see this Fiesta and I ended up buying it. My mum and dad were away at the time because they would have tried to stop me wasting so much money on my first car. I eventually got the price down from £3,800 to £3,200. I gave the Fiesta owner the deposit that day but I couldn't drive so I cleaned and waxed it.

But I soon got bored of the Fiesta and then sold it for £500 profit. Predictably, I wanted something more powerful and expensive. I'd passed my driving test months earlier and often used to drive to work in Hatton Garden on a Saturday and Sunday. On my days off, I'd go down to Southend with some mates. I started looking around for something flashier, even though I wasn't exactly flush with cash. But that never stopped me.

The next big change in my life came when Alan Sugar bought Tottenham Hotspur FC. I went from being this boy with no interest in football to a soccer nut virtually overnight. My grandfather had earlier taken me to watch Leyton Orient v West Ham and there was loads of trouble and that had put me off it for years.

Alan Sugar's purchase of Spurs seemed to be done on impulse rather than for pure business reasons. He was a genuine Spurs fan but he didn't go all the time. After they bought the club, Amstrad got an executive box.

I think Alan bought the club partly because it would have made his father very proud, although he would never have admitted that openly. However, I have no doubts he put his heart and soul into that club as well as many millions of pounds. I think it's awful the way so many so-called supporters claim he was only in it for the money. They have no idea what he and his family went through for that club. I wouldn't have blamed him in the slightest if he'd turned his back on Tottenham because of the way they treated him, but Alan doesn't make a habit of running away from anyone.

Around this time I left the shop in Hatton Garden and started working as a freelance jewellery trader for my father's firm; I was also buying and selling high-value watches. My dad would give me old lines of jewellery and I'd go all over the country selling them into shops. I used to walk in with one big plastic bag, which I then emptied out on the counter. That way it all looked cheaper and was easier to sell.

Another reason I'd got interested in football again (besides Alan Sugar) was because a Spurs player called Vinnie Samways came to me wanting to buy a watch, so I arranged to meet him at the Tottenham training ground at Mill Hill one weekday afternoon. It was a right dump, nothing much more than a shed on a field. I went over to say hello to Gary Lineker in the canteen and he completely blanked me. Vinnie Samways eventually bought a Rolex off me, which then got me access to the other Spurs players at that time and many of them started calling on my 'services'.

At that time, I used to meet the players at TGI's in Mill Hill. Spurs players Paul Gascoigne, Justin Edinburgh and Gary Mabbutt were often there. Then I began going to the Spurs away games with the Sugars in Alan's Rolls-Royce with his driver. At other times, I would drive them in Alan's Range Rover. If we travelled beyond Birmingham, Alan would hire a plane and we'd fly from a tiny airfield near Chigwell. It was often bumpy and terrifying up in that small plane, but Alan was a qualified pilot so he'd just sit there reading the paper not in the least bit bothered, while Louise (Alan's daughter), Simon, Daniel, Ann and I would all be shitting ourselves wondering what the hell we were doing travelling on the plane.

At most away games, people were reasonably nice to Alan, but at home games it often got pretty nasty. We were in the limo once when this bloke just stuck his head in the door and began swearing at us and we pushed him out. But Alan was not frightened of anyone and he was up for a fight with most of these people. When he clashed with Spurs manager Terry Venables, he went through hell in the papers because people accused him of financially killing the club. Player Neil Ruddock's wife organised a protest outside Alan's house. On another occasion, someone broke into the grounds of his home and prised open the garage doors and scratched the word 'CUNT' on to Alan's blue Rolls-Royce. He got 2,000 hate-mail letters every week. But he shrugged it all off and just got on with it. That's the Sugar way.

Alan's family begged him to quit Spurs. Simon never used to say much about it but it had a bad effect on Daniel, and Louise was distraught to see her father going through hell. I had a good relationship with Lou: she is a remarkable girl with a huge heart and a massive love for her family. But Alan genuinely wanted them to win the league; he wanted Spurs to become as successful as Manchester United. When Spurs finally won their way back into the FA Cup, the fans sang for Alan and I think that was a pivotal moment because it made him feel appreciated. After all, Spurs had earlier had 12 points deducted and been banned from the FA Cup for a season. Ultimately, Alan changed the face of football by manufacturing Sky boxes. But it was no surprise when he pulled out of Spurs. He'd had enough.

As part of the work deal with my dad, I set up a company called

Maison D'Or to use the end-of-line jewellery and watches from my dad and sell them off at good prices. My dad couldn't sell direct to retailers, but the Nineties saw a lot of changes and the wholesalers were becoming dinosaurs because the independents were dealing direct with the manufacturer.

Having spotted the hole in the market, I was also keen not to be labelled as just working for my dad. He'd wanted me to set up an arm but I insisted I did it on my own, and he was all right about that in the end. My first few months in my new repping job were spent driving around the entire UK. I was more than happy to criss-cross the country to make a buck.

I'd walk into a jeweller's and say I was from Maison D'Or and I had some end-of-line stuff to show them. A lot of them reacted quite badly to me and they were very rude, but I had a 90 per cent success rate at selling over a period of a year, so I didn't care about the idiots.

I worked on a freelance commission, so for every £1,000 sale I earned £100. I made quite a lot of money but I did have a lot of expenses to pay for, although I was also making extra money selling my watches to lots of the Chigwell 'set' at the same time. A customer would ask me how much it would cost for me to get them a certain watch – say a Cartier Panther – and then I'd go and get it for them. I'd then phone around the retailers and they'd say I could have 30 per cent off and I'd tell the customer 25 per cent and keep the 5 per cent as a fee. On a ten-grand watch, it wasn't a bad result.

It all seemed to be going very well and my turnover

eventually topped half-a-million pounds over three years. One of my biggest customers was a bloke called Neil who ended up buying me out because he then saved himself the 5 per cent mark-up. But it was a great deal for me because he paid me £100,000 for the business.

I had to stop selling watches for a year due to the clause in the contract when I sold the company, so I became my dad's official rep, although I was still on commission only. It suited me; I liked having an incentive.

That £100,000 naturally burned a huge hole in my pocket. I ended up spending it on cars and clothes and holidays and all sorts of silly stuff. It only lasted me a couple of months, which was complete madness. I was developing a reckless attitude towards money and nothing would stop me.

When I was 20ish, I accompanied the Sugars on a chartered yacht in the Med just before Simon's wedding; I was due to be his best man. One evening, Alan called me into a room for a chat because he wanted to hear what my best man's speech was going to be about. I knew Alan was brilliant at making speeches but luckily he seemed to like the sound of mine. Then he asked me a favour: 'Would you mind adding some things about my missus Ann?' I was happy to oblige.

I remember singer Tommy Steele (a guest at the wedding) explained to me that, when you get a laugh with a speech, you mustn't wait for it to die down, you have to throw in another gag at that moment. It was good advice. I did a speech in front of about 400 people and it went down very well. Besides Tommy

Steele, guests included Terry Venables (before his fallout with Alan), Gary Mabbutt, Jeremy Beadle and Gerald Ronson.

The wedding was held at the Sugars' mansion in a massive marquee and it seemed like everyone there was after a cheap watch and jewellery from me. Soon the requests came pouring in: 'Jay, what's the latest watch to have?' ... 'What sort of earrings should I have?' I was like their 'dealer' in a sense. The wives were soon dropping subtle hints to their husbands and then I'd walk over to their table and Alan or whoever would say, 'Oh, gawd, there's Jay. That's going to cost me money.'

That wedding was a complete eye-opener because the marquee was impressive and the Sugars had spent a fortune on it all, and that made me feel like I was part and parcel of that super-rich, money-no-object lifestyle. But I wasn't.

Continually changing cars was another predictable part of this attempt to keep up with my rich friends and their families as well. I wanted to show I was successful like them, so I splashed out fifteen grand for this flash Peugeot. It was a lot of money for a kid to spend. I put the deposit down and the day I got it I was really excited, because I felt this was a step up and would make me fit in even better with all the Chigwell set.

I used to get loads of parking tickets and my dad would go mad about them. I had a really stupid attitude and used to park anywhere. It was as if I was trying to emulate those criminals who used to come to the tiny jeweller's where I worked on Saturdays as a kid. I'd even go into a menswear shop and spend £500 without blinking.

Then I paid £400 for my first mobile phone purely because I wanted to keep up with my friends and get one of those huge brick jobbies. My dad kept saying I didn't need it but I ignored him, as usual. No one really needed a mobile phone back then, but I had to have one. It had a very costly monthly contract and I'd phone my granddad and my parents and everyone on it and tell them I was using it.

By this time, I was already known as a sharp kid with fingers in lots of pies. My parents didn't take any rent off me so I had no overheads and chose to continue living at home. It was ridiculous, really, because if they'd thrown me out I would have had to survive on my own and maybe I wouldn't have wasted so much money.

But on a more personal level I felt I was missing out. My sister was getting married and my best friend had just gone up the aisle. I wasn't even in a proper relationship. For my 21st birthday, my parents had invited all my friends round to the house and my dad gave me this diamond ring that I'd always liked the look of. He'd often made jokes about how he'd let me have it when he died. But when I opened my present and saw it was this ring, I was very upset because he'd told me all of his life that I would only have it when he died and this seemed like a bad omen.

The other sad fact was that a lot of my rich friends had Cartier watches. I'd wanted to wake up on my 21st birthday and find a Cartier in a red box beside my bed. That was what I had dreamed of.

That day, I wouldn't even put the ring on. I just couldn't hide my disappointment, even though it was worth a lot more than a Cartier watch. In the end, we drove over to a jeweller's and got one that afternoon. It cost a couple of grand. But it made me feel a million dollars to have that Cartier on my wrist.

Afterwards, I reacted by going on even bigger spending sprees, even though I hardly had any money. I never wanted to be restricted like that again. Meanwhile, I meticulously polished my souped-up 1900 Peugeot obsessively in the driveway at home every Sunday as if to prove how big and successful I was.

My dad, though, played everything by the book. He never even had any problems with criminals trying to rob his factory but then he did install a good security system. He was always sensible like that. I was surprised no one ever held him up with a gun as he left his factory carrying some of his jewellery. I presumed some disgruntled ex-staff member would come back one day but they never did and that's a testament to my dad, I guess. He was a lot more careful than me and, looking back on it, I should have taken more notice of the way he led his life.

5

PROPOSAL SEALS
THE DEAL

It was around this time I fell in love for the first time and it just happened to be with a non-Jewish girl, which was very awkward in many ways. My parents knew about her but I never brought her home. They just ignored her existence, which was ridiculous, but that's how it was back then.

I was already eating out at the best restaurants in the West End, even though I was basically potless, and I guess this must have impressed my first true love. I remember Jack Nicholson being in one place and he wouldn't stop staring at my dinner date, which really pissed me off. Naturally, the girl adored the attention. Mind you, I had just bought her a Cartier watch and lavished designer clothes on her. I'd also just bought myself a BMW worth £25,000, on credit naturally. I was still repping the jewellery and earning good money, but I had also managed to secure a lot of credit from the suppliers. That meant I'd get £5,000 in and spend £5,500.

In the end, this girlfriend went to Thailand for a family holiday and ended up finding another man. At the time I was heartbroken – especially as I was dumped over a long-distance phone call – but we eventually became friends again, and are still friends to this day.

My business at this time went something like this: someone would buy a watch for £1,500 that might be worth £1,300. I would earn £200 out of that. Then I'd get the money and I'd think, 'Oh shit!' because I had to pay a bill, credit card, car insurance, whatever. I was also always getting all these speeding and parking fines and never paying them.

On one occasion, a bailiff turned up at the house and I owed them £500. My dad was the only other person in the house at the time because my mum was at the hospital with my grandfather, who was ill. They said I had to pay £500 cash or I'd be put in a cell. I asked my dad to pay it and he wouldn't. So I got on the phone to my mum and she made my dad pay it, but in hindsight I wish he hadn't. My dad was right and my mum was wrong. I got away with it yet again because there was no way she would let me be dragged off to a cell. While I know it may sound like I am being harsh on my mum, she loved me in such an unconditional way she always wanted to help me, although long term it may have helped me if she hadn't.

One week, I'd earn £1,000, the next week £2,000 and the

week after that £100; I was using the cash to fund my lifestyle, instead of building up the stock for the business, or investing in a property.

I kept thinking that a really big deal would come along soon. My bank manager knew my dad and he was like a family friend and he offered me a £10,000 overdraft, which was like a red rag to a bull. The bank manager seemed to think that we were loaded. So I got a £10,000 overdraft, but within weeks I'd spent it all. Then all of a sudden the bank manager left and all my cheques started bouncing.

Then I had a stroke of good luck; I got an opportunity to be part of a retail jewellery shop on Bond Street, in the middle of the West End. The site belonged to the mother-in-law of my friend Simon and she gave it to us and we turned it into a lucrative jewellery and watch business.

I was still living at home but now I had this office and shop in Bond Street, even though I was still repping. We had a phenomenal first year but, after that, Simon's mother-in-law took the shop back and we were stuffed. I was straight back in a big hole of debt within weeks. It would have made more sense if I had a coke addiction or was a drunk. But I was hooked on money and it was costing me dearly.

And in the middle of all this, I was still being ridiculously generous to other people. I bought a second-hand car with my grandfather because he loved to earn money and we were going to sell it on for a profit. I gave him £300 'profit' from the deal just to make him feel better, while, in fact, I sold it for a loss. My whole family loved Barbra Streisand, so I bought them all tickets and ended up spending more than two grand.

I then spent another two grand on a Club class ticket to the States, even though I was stony broke. How did I pay for it? I'd managed to get a new bank account by this time with yet another overdraft on it. I was applying for and getting new credit cards on a weekly basis with credit limits from £5,000 to £25,000. I even had an AmEx gold card that only seriously rich people are supposed to have, even though I wasn't remotely in that category. I overspent on that, so they upgraded the gold card to a platinum card. I would only buy Ralph Lauren, Hugo Boss and Armani clothes. I was living a fantasy life surrounded by people who presumed I was a runaway success.

One of my friends couldn't afford to go skiing so I topped him up by a grand and I never even asked him for the money back. Meanwhile, my dad was getting angrier and angrier with me. Most mornings, I'd try to get out of bed really early and rush downstairs to grab the post before he saw all my bills.

My car was towed away and wheel-clamped regularly but I'd just take out another credit card and pay it off. If only I had not been able to get all that credit in the first place. Often, I'd just think to myself, 'How do I get through this week?' and then an order would come in for some watches and I'd be just saved. I'd sell them on and drip feed payments to the suppliers. They all thought I was 'OK' because of my dad being a well-known jeweller.

In the middle of all this, I kept a close eye on the so-called

'Chigwell jet-set' headed up by men in their forties, who were mostly into property. They all adored Maggie Thatcher because she had made them rich. My mum and dad were definitely not part of that scene. The 'jet-set' members had to belong to a tennis club or even own their own tennis court. They all had brand-new Rollers and their wives had Merc convertibles. The women had to have the latest Rolexes and the even wealthier ones had diamonds in theirs. The men favoured yellow-gold Rolexes. Everything was for show. All of the men wore Gucci loafers and had their suits hand-made abroad, *not* in Savile Row. Meanwhile, the wives would waste their husbands' money in the nearest Armani store.

A couple of these high-profile characters went to prison for fraud and stuff like that. There was this one guy who took the can for a lot of them and all these big names supported that same man's family. I saw the sign – 'JEW IN TROUBLE' – and heard how all his rich and famous mates were rallying round to help him. I was another Jew rapidly spiralling into similarly big trouble. Would they help me as easily? I was not being helped at that time as I had nothing on those people who weren't connected with my business.

By this time, I was spending at least £100,000 a year and only earning £50,000 and paying tax. As the financial pressure started to mount on me, I was walking along Chigwell parade when I spotted this stunning blonde sitting on the green opposite the shops and, as I got closer to her, I realised it was Nicole, whom I'd dated almost seven years earlier. My jaw truly hit the floor because I realised instantly that I had to be with her. I sat down and spoke to her for about two hours and it really was love at second sight. This was the person I was going to marry.

Nicole was still seeing some guy from Southend at the time so nothing much happened initially. But I knew the guy was not treating her well and she soon called it a day with him. But it wasn't easy to convince Nicole I was the guy for her after the way I had dumped her all those years earlier. So, for the next two years, we remained close friends and had the occasional snog but nothing more. I guess we were holding back our true feelings for each other.

Then, one Christmas, Nicole was about to head off to Miami with her parents and I got incredibly insecure and convinced myself she was going to meet someone else. I even told her as much just before she departed, although naturally I hoped she would miss me so much that we'd get together properly on her return. But, instead, she met an incredibly rich guy from New York and fell in love with him and moved to the States and got engaged!

Back in the UK, I was gutted when I heard the news, although I kept telling her in long phone calls that I knew we would end up together. Eventually, she broke off the engagement and we finally got together properly. At that time, I moved into a house with a mate of mine whose marriage had broken up suddenly, so I then went and neglected Nic again. When I went off for a boys-only holiday in Florida with Daniel Sugar, she got really mad and that was when I realised I had to come home and marry her.

I was still selling jewellery and watches. By now, I had my own office in my dad's place but my debts to the suppliers were mounting at an alarming rate.

I took Nicole to Gibraltar on a work trip and we stayed at my family's flat in Marbella. It was Friday and there was this beauty spot called The Rock, where you sit at the end of the beach, and I was going to propose to Nicole on that rock. But the night before we went there, we were in a local restaurant and bumped into Ann and Alan Sugar and their friends. They spent the night winding me up about why I had not yet proposed to Nicole – if they only knew what my intentions were! The next day, we were invited on to Alan's yacht, so I decided I'd propose to Nic on the boat.

I ended up getting so drunk that I couldn't actually blurt out the proposal. I remember walking off the boat with Nicole and the port was spinning. I told Nicole to take me to my friend Simon's restaurant as I knew he would have a solution to my drunken state. The next day, we got to Gibraltar Airport and Nicole was about to get on the plane when I said, 'Will you marry me?'

When she said, 'Yes,' I was thrilled but, to be honest, I really regret the way I proposed. She deserved better.

I then had to phone her dad to ask for her hand. He was fine about it all and then I phoned my mum and she said, 'Lovely,' but she told me to call my dad. All he said was 'Oh'. Meanwhile, Nic was on the plane back to London.

It should have been the happiest day of my life but, just after speaking to my family, I got a call from my bank, who were foreclosing on me. I was in deep trouble. I also owed my dad money. I needed £25,000 to get out of this latest hole.

I'd long since become a master at looking as if everything was OK. I called it the 'man in the mirror syndrome'. I simply never told anyone what was happening. But I was already on a non-stop runaway train. The only light at the end of the tunnel was my family and I was praying that they wouldn't let the train crash.

I'd bought my first house in Loughton for £88,000 and sold it not long afterwards for £98,000. Then I bought a four-bed house in Chigwell for £165,000 and did it up and sold it for nearly £400,000 a couple of years later. In the middle of all this, my debts were mounting. Everyone around me seemed to be spending without any fears about debt. I got caught up in that whole mentality. Getting that first mortgage was easy because my money problems were only just coming to the surface and, back then, virtually anyone could get a home loan, not like today. I'd got a mortgage by bullshitting about my earnings; everyone did it in those days. I also bought a dog for £400, which was stupid, and splashed out on yet another car – this time the latest BMW 330 Coupé – worth thirty grand.

I desperately needed another lucrative string to my bow and thought about what I wanted to do, before eventually settling on becoming a football agent. It made sense as I already had lots of contacts in the football world through selling watches, although I didn't have the FIFA licence that you needed back then. Neither did I have the €100,000 you needed to log with FIFA, so I joined up with PMS Sports. My partner then was a property agent and had good contacts with London clubs but not with the players, so it was a good partnership.

I ended up being a partner in that business for a few years. We had an office in Woodford. My partner had a FIFA badge so it was all perfectly legit. We soon had stars like Paolo Di Canio of West Ham and Ramon Vega of Spurs among my big names. I quickly made £150,000 on one deal and so naturally I went out and got myself a Porsche. I met loads of young footballers and we signed up a total of 150 players, which may sound a lot but many of them were not big-hitters by any means. I eventually made a total of £200,000, which got me a little way out of the hole but I needed to make a lot more than that in order to start really chipping away at my debts.

Then disaster struck and the smaller clubs stopped buying the younger players and the money dried up virtually overnight. The Bosman rule changed the face of football because it meant that players who were out of contract could effectively be transferred for free, so there was no commission in it for agents like me. Only the major clubs spent big money and we needed the bread and butter deals to survive. I took Spurs' star striker Les Ferdinand to Italy possibly to sign for Brescia and we even went to an AC Milan match. But, although Brescia offered big money, the deal never materialised and a year later he went to West Ham instead. Les had been very happy at Spurs; it was the club he'd supported as a child. However, the problem was that the then manager Glenn Hoddle didn't play him enough.

I was finding out the hard way that trying to be a football agent wasn't as easy as it had first appeared and I soon slipped back into the watch business because at least I knew where I stood. Or so I thought.

6

SWIMMING
WITH SHARKS

Nicole and I went to the States for a holiday and we came to find ourselves lying on sun loungers by the pool in the five-star Ritz-Carlton, Florida. I was wearing a Rolex Daytona, which was rare, and this American next to us said he liked my watch so I got talking to him about how I was a watch dealer in London. A new Daytona with a green leather strap and a green face had just come out and I happened to have one at home.

This American said he wanted it. It was eight grand and he wired the money by the time I got home. I sent the watch out to him and then he introduced me to one of his school friends. He was the investor in his watch business and I eventually sold them dozens of watches and it worked brilliantly well because the dollar was so weak. Once again, I had a stroke of luck at just the right moment and was saved from complete extinction. But, as ever, I was skating on ever thinning ice.

Then the American watch deal came crashing to an end because the prices of watches in the States plummeted thanks to the sinking dollar. So yet another business died a death and I'd already started borrowing heavily against it.

I had concentrated so much on the American side of things that I had neglected my UK watch and jewellery business. Up until then, I'd been just about paying the interest on my loans but now I had a cash-flow problem in *all* directions.

When I eventually married Nicole in 1998, we had wedding gifts of about nine grand in money, which all went into our joint bank account, and I used all the money to pay the interest on loans. No one in the family had a clue what I was doing. I used that money to pay off credit cards and stuff like that. I remember one day, just a few weeks after we got married, looking in our joint bank account and realising that basically I had no money in it.

At that point, I was working in an office above my dad's jewellery shop and I can remember Nicole ringing me and going mad at me over the phone. 'Where has all our money gone?'

But I never told her the truth. I brushed it all off as I was so good at doing. 'What are you worried about?' I told her. 'I just move money around. There'll be some back in the account soon.' Then I said, 'How do you think we pay for this lifestyle?'

You see, I was on this merry-go-round that meant I could take money from the business account and put it back into the joint account. That's when Nicole backed right off. She didn't work and I was already giving her a good life and she enjoyed lots of luxuries. After that, she never really questioned where it was all coming from but, of course, the problem was that I was overspending in all departments.

The strange thing with me was that, although I used the money from the joint account, I did always replace it. I would juggle all my balls in the air. A classic example was to write cheques that I knew would bounce but it would give me some extra days – in other words, breathing space – for money to come in from sales. The problem was that I used the company money. That meant I was living on turnover and not profit, which is suicide.

I knew the only way I could earn any consistent money was to get some watch stock and stick to what I knew best. But I didn't even have the money to buy any watches at this stage.

Then a guy I'd first met all those years earlier when I was a kid in that Chigwell jeweller's got in touch with me out of the blue. His name was Mark and he was after a £10,000 loan. Now you might wonder why he'd come to me, but I knew that, if I could scrape the money together for him, then he could help me with some much bigger loans after I had proved myself to him.

I was absolutely right. Mark paid that £10,000 back to me very quickly and then I knew he would lend me bigger bucks. How twisted is that? Being offered that cash would be a big result. That shows what a fool I was. But I signed up for it because I had no choice. None of the legitimate sources of money like the banks or the credit card companies would come near me any more.

So the first fifty grand I borrowed off Mark went into paying off some of my debts immediately and then I borrowed more money to buy a hundred grand's worth of watches and I was soon making money again. Mark would eventually open the door to more new 'saviours' who would lend me money.

I have never forgotten that day when he gave me my first big loan of £100,000. It really was the beginning of the end for me when I look back on it. I sat down in Mark's house and asked him if he had access to money and he said he lent money to car dealers and got interest on it. I said I was in a position to borrow money from him and I could pay him interest on that money. I asked him what interest and he said 1 per cent a week, which is obviously 4 per cent a month.

I said, 'If I needed a hundred grand on Friday, how quickly could you put it up?'

'Within 24 hours.'

So I waited four or five days and then I phoned him back and said, 'I have a deal on the table and I need a hundred grand. You can have the money back in a week.'

His fee was five grand on it for a week's loan; that's 5 per cent in a week. I took the money and paid him back the £105,000 within the week.

What really happened was that I gave the full £100,000 to a watch supplier I owed the money to, and then got more credit on the watches in order to pay Mark back. Now I had Mark's confidence because I had paid him back that money on time.

But with the US dollar crashing, things were falling apart all around me. I soon started underselling my watch stock to pay the interest on new loans and then I had no choice but to borrow more money. I wasn't involved with nasty gangsters yet, although that original lender Mark was a heavy sort of character, who'd been in the nightclub business with some notorious north London gangsters. I was getting incredibly reckless.

Mark had no idea there was a problem because I'd paid him the interest so quickly on that first loan. Soon I'd be borrowing money from other people to make these payments to him for other loans, including from Nicole's parents. Much of the time I would invent fictitious deals to persuade people to lend me money.

That's when my oldest friend, Jonathan, first appeared on the scene as a lender. In truth, he should have pulled me to one side there and then and asked if I was in trouble. But, like most of us, he was just looking for a quick buck. He lent me forty grand, and earned back four grand after two or three weeks because I needed it urgently and, just like Mark, I wanted to prove to him that I was 'good for it'. Jonathan was so happy with the interest payment he bought me a present, which turned out to be a Tiffany vase worth hundreds of pounds. In retrospect, he should have seen I was in trouble and helped, rather than insisting on taking mad amounts of interest.

So one of my best friends was now hooked in and I knew he'd be good for anything from £50,000 to £200,000. With Jonathan, I'd simply phone him up and borrow on 10 per cent interest short term. He loved it because I gave him that interest in cash. I was already dancing around in a financial desert. God knows why, but I just couldn't seem to bring myself to tell him the truth. What was it inside me that stopped me from telling him what was really happening?

Then Jonathan lent me £100,000 and I agreed to pay him £5,000 interest but, in order to give him his money back plus interest, I had to borrow another £100,000, this time from my very close friend Lucas. Then Jonathan lent me £120,000 and I paid that to Lucas. Round and round I started going.

I was playing Jonathan and Lucas off each other but they had no idea of this. I was gaining their confidence to hit them for more and more loans. It would only become a problem if I was late paying them back, which, of course, would inevitably happen. That's when I realised I had to give that original money-lender Mark all this cash back. After months of juggling, I was already sinking deeper and deeper into the shit, so I had to bring another person in to keep this all going.

He was a criminal called Den White, who was a right Essex hardnut, and had been told about me by a so-called mate of mine. Now I had really stepped over the line and headfirst into the underworld. I said I had a 'special deal' for him.

'How about £160,000?' I said to him, without batting an eyelid.

The next day, Den turned up with the total amount in readies. The money-lenders were gathering like vultures. The word was out that I was there for the taking. If I could pay my friend Jonathan back, then I could stay in business, but the trouble was I would have to pay Den £16,000 a month interest for that £160,000 loan.

Still no one at home realised I was in it up to my neck. I still had the Porsche outside my office and the lenders would come to my office and see all the watches. They didn't stop and think how I could be earning enough money to pay these debts. As long as I kept everyone happy, I could keep getting these loans. But I was losing thousands of pounds a week because all I was doing was paying interest.

Then I started juggling with my friend Lee's money. I had known Lee for many years as he'd been one of my watch customers, and he'd come to my wedding. He'd bought a lot of watches off me; I used to take them to his house and he would have all the new models. I'd be out with Lee and he'd say, 'Have you got ten grand?' and I'd say, 'Yeah,' and then I'd get it from my office for him and he would do the same thing for me.

I'd eventually even rent an office from him. Before that, I had been operating out of the third ownership of the jewellery shop in Romford and worked out of an office there.

Then, one day, Lee said to me, 'If I gave you £150,000, what sort of return would you give me?'

We agreed 6 per cent a month on £150,000 and that was the first time I got into a commitment of borrowing money from him. He gave me the money in cash when we met in the street in Romford in 2001.

So now I owed Lee £9,000 a month. It didn't seem like a lot of money now I had £150,000 to spend on watches to sell, which meant I would make about £25,000 a month. It didn't seem so bad back then.

But, looking back on it now, the truth is I was already losing my mind. It was all Monopoly money in a sense and I was being pulled further and further into the hole.

Lee had seen that I was struggling with bills and all the pressure I was under. One of the problems back then was that I'd have to pay for the watches and then not see any return in my account for the next two to four weeks.

I put Lee's loan in to stock, which allowed me to get up to date with my suppliers and buy watches. The business was still generating £1 million a year turnover at that time, which meant I was earning £100,000 a year.

But a hundred grand was only really sixty grand after tax, and I was spending at least forty grand more on cars and mortgages and stuff, not to mention what I owed these illegal loan sharks in interest payments alone. So that £150,000 loan from Lee gave me some breathing space. Of course, he presumed I'd just buy stock with it, but the truth is I used it to pay other people off.

And I was still spending too much on holidays – a minimum of £25,000. I had over £100,000 in cars for me and Nic, and we were spending £10,000 a month on the house, holidays, entertainment and clothes. I was living in a half-a-million-pound house, which had a £300,000 mortgage on it.

I immediately took out more credit with the watch suppliers, but after paying off that nine grand a month to Lee, I had little or nothing left. But at least I now had some stock, so I reckoned I'd make some money.

Even the birth of my daughter Arabella cost me six grand for private fees at the exclusive Portland Hospital.

Initially, I just about coped with servicing those payments for the first six months. But every month it was getting harder and harder. I always had to give Lee cash and he owned the office I was using. But he then told his mates how good I was at paying the interest payments, so they started pressing to lend me more cash.

Lender Den White had been a friend of Lee's and he was also buying watches off me. Although he was a friendly enough character, I knew if I crossed him my future on this earth might be rather limited.

It was when I was really struggling to find the nine grand interest payment to Lee that I looked to Den for more money. I even made out I had this business deal with Lee and asked him if he would be interested in 'investing' some cash with me. It was all a lie.

And, in the middle of all this, I bought my secretary a BMW convertible and partnered my dad in buying a Bentley Turbo R. He thought we'd gone 50/50 on it, but I had lied to him and actually put more money into it. I wanted to keep proving what a success I was, but it was all funded through money borrowed from these evil characters.

Straight away, Den coughed up £20,000 for 10 per cent a month. So for the first three months, it was £2,000 a month. But all that £20,000 did was pay for two months of interest payments to Lee, and it gave me some other money to pay off mortgages and credit card bills.

So I had to keep paying them both. Then, after a couple more months, I asked Den if he wanted to put up any more money. He was over the moon; he came up with £150,000. I was a bit naïve and thought he was trying to help me but he was charging 10 per cent interest a month, so he was only helping himself. He didn't need to say what would happen if I didn't pay. I knew Den was a criminal and he was well respected. I was going completely against the grain; I was now dealing with out and out criminals. I'd crossed the line in every sense now.

By now, I was waking up on Monday mornings and trying to work out how to get to Friday without taking out another loan. It had escalated so fast that I was already paying out £120,000 a week ... *in interest*! Only a few months earlier, it had seemed to be around ten grand. 'Shit!' I remember thinking to myself. 'This is completely out of control.'

Yet, in the middle of all this, I developed the most incredible inner karma. I was in denial and I had this way of staying calm and dealing with all my problems and then coming home at night and not hinting at any of my problems to my family. I still told no one of my financial nightmare. Why the fuck not? I owed hundreds of thousands to a bunch of evil criminals.

Everything was going up and up in interest. I was sweating every day and not sleeping but always coming home with a smile on my face.

This was yet another turning point in my life ... and everything was about to go from bad to worse.

7
DEATH AND TAXES

One day, my mate Lee – to whom I now owed a huge wedge of cash – phoned me and said, 'I need to talk to you. I'm comin' over.'

We lived two minutes from each other so I thought nothing of it when he rang. I went outside and waited for him. He turned up in his Bentley Azure and I wandered over to him as the electric window on the passenger side rolled smoothly down.

'What's up?'

He looked at me but said nothing at first, and then I noticed a massive sports bag next to him on the passenger seat.

'I need you to put this somewhere safe just for tonight.'

I leaned further into the car as he unzipped the bag for a moment to let me see what was in it. It was crammed full of notes.

'Fuck me. How much is in there?' I pulled back and gulped the air.

'Best part of two million quid,' said Lee as cool as a cucumber.

Lee then zipped up the bag, picked it up and got out of the Bentley.

We walked into my garage and he opened the boot of my BMW and put it straight in.

I said, 'What's this all about?'

'Don't worry. It's nothing major. I'll explain it all to you tomorrow.'

Then he drove off.

I felt a little bit shocked and vulnerable at that moment because it was the first time I realised that Lee was involved in bad stuff.

I know … I know. I should have refused to help him but he had me over a barrel with all those loans. I was being sucked into a criminal netherworld I knew little about.

I walked back in the house that night in a bit of a daze. It was yet another pivotal moment because I had no choice but to play along. This was the reality of the risk of borrowing money from gangsters; now they owned me.

Nicole naturally wanted to know what was happening after she'd seen Lee pull up in the Bentley. Lee had become part of the family, and Nicole used to cook for him most nights. He'd even stayed at our house when his flat was being done up. What surprised my wife most was that Lee had arrived in the car but had never come in to say hello.

'So what was that all about?' she asked.

'I don't know but Lee has just put a shitload of money in my car.'

'How much?'

'I really don't know,' I said, 'but it's a lot.' Obviously, I was trying to play it all down. 'Come and have a look.'

So Nic and I went into the garage together, opened the boot of the BMW and unzipped the bag.

'Oh my God … that's a lot of money!' whispered Nic.

Neither of us had ever seen so much cash before in our lives.

Then we closed the bag, shut the boot and went back into the kitchen.

We both talked about the money for ages that night. We didn't want to believe it was connected to something serious like drugs, and we convinced ourselves we were just helping out a friend. But, in my heart of hearts, I knew that wasn't the case. I hadn't done anything wrong in my life, so, if the police turned up, I'd just tell them a friend of mine popped round and left it with me. But I knew perfectly well that, if the police did find that cash, I'd probably end up in prison. I was really just deluding myself.

It turned out Lee believed he was about to be raided by the police and he didn't want the cash to be found, so he gave it to me. I was deemed to be a straight guy who wouldn't be touched by the cops.

In any case, I'd always had this very carefree attitude. Lee knew I was never nervous about putting big amounts of money into the bank or carrying it about, so I guess he figured I could handle looking after that money for him.

I held on to that money for about 15 hours and then Lee came and picked it up. Now I had 'passed' another 'test', which meant that I was 'good' for another loan. I never once was tempted to take that money and use it to help bail myself out because I knew I'd be signing my own death warrant if I'd done that.

Lee called first thing the next morning to say he was popping over and, at 7.30am, he turned up and took the bag back in the very same Bentley he'd been in the previous evening.

We were good friends so I didn't expect a bung for it. He was like a brother to me, and this made us even stronger; we spent most days together and went to watch all the Spurs home games. He, in many ways, was the brother I'd always wanted, and we totally had each other's back.

Later that same day, I saw Lee at his office and asked him what the cash in the bag was all about. He said someone who lived in his flat had had a problem with the police. I found out later that the person got nicked and Lee kept the money for himself, although he allegedly paid the jailed man back years later.

But there were obviously troubling elements to Lee; besides being involved with some shady characters, he was overweight and dealt with his weight issues by spending money like a maniac, even compared with me. In a Gucci shop in Spain once, he tried on one shoe in a shop and then bought them in every colour. It cost him thousands. He did the same with anything that fitted him.

But looking after that money worked in one sense because, soon afterwards, Lee lent me another £150,000 and I agreed 6 per cent a month interest. Lee believed I needed the money because of a cash-flow problem with my watch business.

A couple of months later, a car dealer called Mike West contacted me. He'd known me for many years and knew I would be up for a money-making deal and said he had a deal for me that might help make us some money. He had no idea how much shit I was in.

He told me he was representing these people who wanted a UK-based company to sell some diamonds through and I had a company, which would be ideal. I didn't question what they were really up to. I just saw it as a huge deal with a lot of turnover and a 4 per cent profit, which would give me £40,000 for every million pounds they put through my company. To me, it was just another stroke of luck. When you are as desperate as I was, you only ever look at the up-side.

I had known Mike and his brother for many years through their involvement in their father's business. In truth, I never trusted Mike, but I liked him as a person because he was quite a character.

But Mike had a tendency to push his luck. He had a BMW 5 series at the time my dad was about to buy a new Merc for my mum. Mike then asked my dad to part-exchange the BMW with the dealer Dad was about to get the Merc from. I asked him if the car was 100 per cent straight and he looked me in the eye and insisted it was. As a result, I helped him out and asked my dad to do the deal for him. A few weeks later, the Merc dealer came back to us hopping mad because the BMW had had its clock turned back by 50,000 miles. To add to our embarrassment, the Merc dealer had been recommended by a close family friend, so you can imagine how they felt.

Mike had made me and my dad look like a right pair of crooks, while he didn't seem to give a toss. But, in the end, he did finally sort it all out, so I didn't fall out with him and we often referred each other to business 'opportunities'.

Then Mike set me up with a meeting with a guy in his mid-fifties called John so we could go through the 'fine print' of the diamonds deal. John was driving a silver R4 Audi and I met him in a park at Woodford Bridge. Middleman Mike was there as well and the whole thing felt more like a dodgy drugs deal because it was so cloak and dagger. That should have set the alarm bells ringing, I suppose, but I wasn't in the frame of mind to walk away from anything which might pay me forty grand a week. I quickly agreed with this guy John that I would do the deal through my business, but I said all the diamond money had to come in one lump because I didn't do part payments. He agreed immediately and it all seemed to go very smoothly.

John also said the money would be put into my company account immediately. This all happened on a Friday and, within hours, £1 million turned up in my account. It should have been £1.2 million under the terms of our agreement, so already £200,000 was missing. So I went back to John and said that it *all* had to go in, otherwise I would not send out the money.

After the money arrived, I was meant to send it on to the seller but I refused to do so as it wasn't there in its entirety – I wasn't going to do part payments. The middlemen, John and Mike West, didn't have a problem with what I was doing and told me to hold on to the money until the balance arrived.

I went home on that Friday night feeling rather good until my mobile rang at about 9.00pm. The guy on the other end was particularly abusive, telling me not to fuck around with his money. He told me that, come 9.00am on Monday morning, if the money wasn't with him, he would send two of his colleagues around to pay me a visit.

At this point, I decided to phone my friend Den. Den knew everyone, from the people who ran the streets right up to royalty. He was a good contact to have, as he was able to sell watches to people I could not get to. I explained my predicament about the Mr Big who had phoned me and, true to his word, he called me back within an hour and, from that point on, became the broker between me and this guy.

He assured me it would all be there by Monday at the latest, so at that point I presumed everything was fine. I got home that night in quite a good mood because I believed I had earned £40,000 (which was my handling fee) and all I'd had to do was meet some bloke in a car park. They'd talked about two or three big deals a week so I could at least see myself making headway, moneywise.

On the day of that first deal, I got to the office and there was a fax there from a company in Dubai saying that they would like to buy diamonds off me to a value of a million quid. It was as sweet as that. Then they gave me the company to buy the diamonds from, and the buyer paid me for the stones once I issued the invoice. Then I paid the supplier, I then booked a courier company to collect the stones and deliver them to my customer in Dubai. I said I had the stones, and all I had to do was send an invoice to that company in Dubai, it was that simple.

So we started doing deals on a regular basis. I would get £100,000 and then send £80,000 out and so on. It kept going for a while but there was a problem – I was funding the VAT on each deal, but, due to all the other stress I had financing all the other loans, I simply couldn't see that. The diamond guys were meant to be funding the VAT, but they weren't, so in fact I was borrowing more money from more sharks at a ridiculous rate just to keep funding the VAT, which had never been my responsibility. It got to the stage where it seemed like I owed them over £1 million, although I didn't, as the million-plus was the VAT I had already paid. But they refused to see it that way, and said it was down to me. I had been well and truly mugged.

It later emerged that the guy at the top was blowing millions of pounds on his own lifestyle and was using me as a smokescreen. Again, my problem was I was under so much pressure I just could not see it. And it's a real shame that I didn't clock the fact, because, had I listened to my team around me and stopped panicking, I would have ended up making millions of pounds.

The guys behind the scheme were Indians and they started harassing me quite nastily. I wasn't in a complete panic yet because I had some watch stock to duck and dive with, but I'd made a very bad decision by not thinking about the whole question of VAT.

I was desperate to get some money and I just thought they needed a solid company. I really didn't realise they were all crooks and simply needed a straight company. Now you might rightly say, how could I be so naïve? As I said earlier, I was desperate. I only heard what I wanted to hear. My world was caving in with debt, so I convinced myself that maybe this diamond scheme would rescue me.

The characters would give me a customer in England and then insisted that all I was doing was buying off a company and that company would get paid before I paid the company I bought the stock from. But the problem was I had to wait for the rest of the money and that's when the Indians behind the scheme started making threats.

Then it emerged that John who'd set this up was in more trouble than I was. He owed the Indians millions of pounds and was trying to work it back by doing things for them like finding mugs like me to handle their ill-gotten gains. The other major problem was the 'Mr Big' behind it all – he was a compulsive gambler who regularly blew a million pounds in one night in a casino. He was handling diamonds, platinum, mobile phones, and was involved in millions of pounds every day in turnover. This 'Mr Big' even had his own jet.

So this whole deal was quickly turning into a complete disaster. Initially, I wasn't too worried because I thought all that money would eventually come through the door. But, as I said, they were expecting me to pay all their VAT, when, in fact, I did not owe it to them. What a complete mug I had been. Now I didn't know which way to turn. I was going through hell because I'd gone and got 'into bed' with a bunch of gangsters.

I couldn't sleep at nights because I was worried they'd firebomb the house, hurt my wife and kids and then try to finish me off. Nic knew nothing about what was happening because I was still putting on this ridiculous front to her and all the rest of my friends and family.

Then I decided to come clean to my mum, and I told her I was in deep trouble and needed £400,000 right there and then. My parents were astounded. I also told my mum I had even rung wealthy old family friend Cyril Dennis on his mobile in his car and pleaded with him. 'I'm in trouble ... I'm in trouble ... Cyril, you gotta help me.'

He didn't know what to say in response. Hardly surprising, is it?

I was 33 years old. I had a beautiful house, a beautiful car, a beautiful wife, two great kids and even a Filipino maid; we had regular holidays abroad, all the watches and jewellery we wanted. To the outside world, I was a big success story but it was all a façade. The real me was falling apart at the seams. In my head, everything was fine; I could not see the writing on the wall. Only now, in the process of writing this book, can I truly see how much I did wrong.

I'd believed that 'diamond deal' would be my saviour but it was proving to be my downfall. I was now owed the 17.5 per cent VAT I had paid on all the money. It was a nightmare. But, even in my darkest moments, I still believed that eventually I'd come out minted. I convinced myself I would be paid my million quid in VAT and that then I'd be laughing. But – surprise, surprise – the VAT people then decided to investigate me.

They were wondering how, with less than £1 million in annual turnover, I could suddenly expand to £6–£7 million in the space of three months. How stupid was I? I was in deep shit now, not just with gangsters but with the bloody VAT men as well, which in many ways was worse.

Mind you, I still wasn't that worried because I had not done anything actually illegal. As ever, I thought it would all be fine. I'd always looked at it that people might be suspicious but that wasn't my concern. I was there to make money. I hadn't done anything wrong in my eyes. I wasn't buying and selling drugs; I was dealing in legit diamonds. But the VAT people were on my back. They came and looked at my books and I kept saying to them there was nothing to hide. They looked far from convinced.

In the meantime, my bank account at Coutts was frozen after the 'diamond boys' put £400,000 into my bank account, which raised all sorts of suspicions. I phoned my bank to see if the money was in and they refused to send the money out but wouldn't tell me why. I swore at them and they told me to go and see a lawyer if I wanted that money.

I phoned the 'diamond boys' immediately to tell them what

had happened and they told me, 'You are a fuckin' liar. Who the hell do you think you are?'

Shit. I was in even more trouble now.

Then they sent one of their men down to my office and I managed to get hold of my cousin Elliot who was a solicitor so we could have an 'official' meeting rather than allow them to get heavy with me.

I got my cousin to confirm to the 'diamond boys' that my account had indeed been frozen and I wasn't bullshitting. I then phoned the bank on my speaker phone in front of the gangsters and got them to repeat what they said earlier. My cousin, in turn, advised me to hire a barrister and then he'd summons Coutts to explain why they wouldn't pay the money out from my account. Naturally, I was desperately trying to prove to these heavy characters why there was a problem, in case they still thought I was trying to con them.

'Now you know it was not me,' I said to them at the end of the meeting. They looked fucking pissed off but they couldn't argue with my 'evidence', thank God.

I then drove up to the West End to see a barrister in his chambers who was going to deal with a Coutts lawyer. The bank still refused to say anything, so we went to court that afternoon to try to force them to release the money.

The Coutts barrister told the judge that my accountant had been suspended by the fraud squad. I didn't know any of this because they would have been breaking the law by telling me. But they had my money and they didn't want to release it.

Then the judge called over my lawyer and we were told the bank wouldn't release the money for another seven days, but I was not worried. It cost me five bloody grand in barristers' fees but at least they knew it was genuine.

But, of course, there were still all those other debts hanging over me. At that time, I'd got interest payments of £68,000 every month.

That's when I decided to draft in another criminal 'face' called Grant; he was a real, old-school gangster from the Seventies who'd first come to me for a six-grand watch he wanted to give his heart specialist. I knew he had access to plenty of cash I could borrow. I went straight in for the kill and got £250,000 off him virtually immediately. I must have been completely bonkers.

Again, that was at 10 per cent a month, which meant interest payments of another £25,000. This was August 2003. So now my monthly interest payments shot up to £93,000. But then it went up to about £100,000 because I also had my mate Jonathan and Lucas to pay back. Then a mate of mine called Rick came in and I soon owed him £300,000, so another £30,000 a month had to go to him. It must sound mind-boggling. So it was now up to £130,000 a month. Talk about Monopoly money!

Oh, and I also owed the mortgage company £11,000 as well on our house. So I borrowed another £25,000 from someone on 10 per cent to pay that off and so it went on and on.

Then the 'diamond boys' – the Indians – came back on the scene yet again. They might have accepted my excuses earlier in the short term but they still wanted their money back and for me to pay their VAT. But they also wanted to put more money through my company so, like the desperate idiot I had become, I agreed.

I should have known better, because all I was really doing was getting deeper and deeper into the shit.

8

SWINGS AND ROUNDABOUTS

One Friday night, I got this phone call from the big boss. It turned out it was his money that had been sent to me that day as part of the latest deal with the other Indians. No one had bothered to tell him I might not be able to pay it back until all the funds had arrived. Jesus, did he scream blue murder at me! He wouldn't let me get a word in edgeways to explain what had happened.

'Listen, you fuckin' Jew fuckin' bastard,' said this voice with a northern accent. 'You've fuckin' got our fuckin' money. Why haven't you paid it on?'

I tried to explain to him yet again that not all the money had been sent to me yet.

He said, 'Don't fuckin' talk to me, you fuckin' Jew cunt.'

There was this rap music going in the background and I think he must have been in a limo going somewhere as he spoke to me.

Then he added, 'You think you can fuck with us? You don't know who the fuck you're dealin' with here. You fuckin' bastard. Someone will be at your fuckin' office at nine on Monday morning and you better fuckin' send that money out. Do you understand what I am fuckin' sayin'?'

I put the phone down without responding and took a very deep breath.

I had no idea who I was really talking to. I was shaking. What had I got myself into? Who are these people? Am I mad? Am I in over my head? What am I going to do?

I got on the phone to Mike West and his mate John who'd kicked off this diamond deal and they seemed unworried and told me the bloke on the phone was off his head on coke and that all would be fine on Monday. And I believed them.

The trouble was that I had stupidly (and typically) used some of that money they'd sent through to pay someone else off and I had no doubt they suspected that. That was why they'd come back at me after all that VAT stuff. They thought I was bullshitting and, to be fair, they had a point.

I knew that, come Monday morning when they paid me a 'visit', I would not have all the money for them. I did not know what to do. Middleman John had warned me they were heavy characters but I never imagined they were this dangerous until I got that call from Mr Big, whoever he was.

I'd told John about that threatening phone call and made it categorically clear that I was not laying out one penny until all the money had been paid. He told me not to worry, and I asked him for a couple of names of who I was dealing with. He refused to give them to me, but at least he accepted my story. If he'd known I was playing for time, it might all have been very different.

Things had got so heavy I needed some form of protection. So I phoned my mate Ali, who is a big, West End character with a lot of muscle when it's needed. Ali is a big, black guy I met through a friend. He used to buy watches and stuff from me. Anyway, I called him and asked him if he had heard of any of these characters and he said, 'How the fuck do you know them? They are my cousins.'

I knew they weren't literally his cousins because they were Indians and he was black, but he then explained they were like family and Ali promised me he would smooth out any problems with them. I was mightily relieved.

But I got Ali to come to the office for that Monday meeting in case there was any trouble. I'll never forget that day in June 2003. It was a hot, sunny day and I was meant to be going on holiday to Venice with my wife and kids the following day.

Middleman John and one of these guys from the Indian 'firm' would also be present. All of them turned up at my office (the one I rented from Lee) in Romford separately. The office was behind a big restaurant, which Lee also owned. It was a nice, modern building next to this huge warehouse. I always kept all my stock at my dad's factory two minutes' drive away because you never knew what might happen with meetings like this.

But at least we all sat down in a civilised manner at first as I calmly explained why I didn't want to send out the money. I said I'd been misled at that first meeting in the car park in Woodford. Just then, a big Merc came sweeping into the car park below the office. Three Indians and a white guy emerged and walked quickly up the back steps to my office and, by the time they walked in, they had guns in their hands. Not good.

One of them saw a picture of my kids on my desk and picked it up. He looked at it for ages before speaking. 'Those your kids?'

I nodded nervously.

'If you want to fuckin' see them again, then you'd better pay us some fuckin' dough.'

I explained I didn't have the money.

But then one of them cut in. 'It's not our problem. You have used our money. We want it back.'

So I had these incredibly heavy characters in my office threatening to kill me. But somehow I still didn't panic, even when they told me I had 24 hours to raise the money.

I begged my friend Lee who owned the office and restaurant to speak to them before they left that day; Lee was better qualified than me in this type of situation due to his own past. They explained to him why I owed them the money. Little did I know I was walking into a classic trap because then Lee offered to lend me the £400,000 to get them off my back. Talk about going further into the 'hole'. Mind you, he gave me that £400,000 interest free. Now you may well ask – why would he do that? He knew the money was coming back and it was a very short-term loan and he took a charge over my home through his own money-lender. They all saw me coming.

I even stupidly thought he was lending me the £400,000 because he was my friend. Yet again, I'd been suckered into taking out another loan. And, remember, he was my office landlord, too. I was owned lock, stock and whatever by Lee.

But the truth is that I would have agreed to anything at the time. Then I did something that perfectly sums up the state of my mind then. I contacted a money-lender called Ash in west London who organised secured loans against people's houses, and got him to lend me some more money, which went straight into my bank account and enabled me still to pay for that holiday in Venice with my family.

And, in the middle of all this, the nasty Indians said that, as long as that £400,000 from Lee came through, they would put another million quid through my business account which meant I would earn a further £40,000. I was actually rather happy to hear it. That's how fucked up I was.

The weekdays were turning into an even worse form of torture for me than they had been previously. I'd leave our house for the office in Romford at 7.00am each morning. I liked that time on my own in the car because it was the only time when I was alone. I knew that the mobile generally wouldn't ring until 9.00am. That meant I was at peace in that car for the only time in the entire day.

Then I got another call from one of the 'diamond boys' I owed that £400,000 to. When I tried to explain it would be with them shortly, thanks to Lee, they turned on me again.

'You're a lying cunt. I don't believe you.'

'Leave me alone,' I pleaded, 'leave me alone.'

'We're going to fuckin' kill you.'

And I was supposed to be going off on holiday with my wife and two young kids later that same day.

It turned out the 'diamond boys' thought I'd got the money back from the VAT people. I even let them see a proof that I'd not had my VAT back yet.

Somehow, I got away with it and ended up in Italy with my family within a few hours. I even managed to unwind on that holiday. We were in this beautiful, five-star resort and I owed millions of pounds. At least I wasn't in the UK, which meant I could avoid all their physical threats but my health was beginning to suffer badly. I seemed to be having heart palpitations. I often shook uncontrollably and I rarely managed more than a few hours' sleep every night. But I didn't tell anyone of my worries.

Lee should have been my saviour but he just added to my downfall because I shouldn't have allowed the Indians to bully me into admitting I owed them that £400,000. I was being fucked over and I should have refused to play ball with them but I was too stressed out to fight anyone.

If I had been living in the real world at that time, I would have either gone to the police or gone to the people who'd lent me all the other money and tried to sort everything out in a friendly, down-to-earth manner. But instead, I just put on a front and pretended everything was fine.

I'd become this person with so much pride that I wouldn't

admit anything to anyone. I suppose it was not much different from a gambling or drug addiction. I didn't wake up one day and just decide I was going to get in this hole; I just let it happen. It was my own fucking fault.

In a sense, I even became addicted to *not* saying I had a problem. I became an even more accomplished liar because I was caught in this cycle of heavy debt involving massive interest payments to characters who would break my legs if I didn't pay them their money. Yet most of the time I was arranging to pay people the following day, knowing full well that I wouldn't have the cash by then.

By this time, Lee was flitting back and forth between Dubai and the UK after he told me the police were looking at him, although he did keep popping back for a few days. I knew he was hiding stuff from me and no doubt he must have found out I was borrowing more money from other people. He even stopped offering me any more money after I'd got that £400,000 from him.

And he had his own set of problems by all accounts. One morning, Lee rang and said a bloke called Pete was on his back and this bloke was talking about how his gang were rivals to a notorious family in north London and were renowned for doing some very scary things to people.

Everything had completely spiralled out of control. My debt to Mark, one of the first people to lend me money, had gone from £100,000 to £200,000 then up to £300,000 then to £400,000 and finally up to £1 million over just six months. It was the stuff of nightmares. I was now supposed to be finding £150,000 a month in interest payments alone. I tried to pay Mark back some through other loans and then I got it down to £250,000 on a rolling basis of 1 per cent a week. Virtually every month I'd ask for another £10,000 to cover some of the interest and he'd then top it up ever further. Now and again, I'd get a lump of money from another lender and pay it all back and start all over again. Although I owed him money, he had made his initial money back in instant payments from me.

Then I'd borrow another £350,000 and start up again, and so it went on and on and on. It was 2003. I'd gone from 0–60 and then from 60mph to about 150mph at high speed, while accelerating into a massive financial disaster. From April to December 2003, I was borrowing money from anyone and everyone who would lend to me.

It all stemmed originally from what was now claimed to be £1.1 million I was owed in VAT because of Mr Big, the other Indians and another rather unpleasant character called Dave. And they were all over me because they wanted a chunk of the VAT money as well.

I also had a good friend in Manchester to whom I owed £470,000 and at least I managed to pay him £400,000 back from another loan. Then £500,000 went to my old boss in Hatton Garden and a few smaller amounts went to other people after I had borrowed yet more money to service those debts. It was a financial merry-go-round which was about to spin out of control.

In hindsight, I should have just fucked off and left the country with what little money I had left. At one stage, I could have held on to £1.5 million I had borrowed and taken my wife and kids to a new life in the sun. But I never once considered it because I wanted to stay with my family in London. In any case, how could I explain to my kids why we couldn't go back to England? And always in the back of my mind was the thought that I would get out of it, somehow.

And this is a measure of how desperate I was. An old mate rang me in that summer of 2003 and asked me to lend him seventy grand. I raised that money immediately from loans from criminals and lent it to him as a mate. Nothing more. But I knew I might have to hit him for a lot more than that one day. To his credit, he paid it back but I never charged him interest on the money he borrowed.

In the meantime, I was getting more and more threats against myself and my family. Everything seemed to be on the verge of turning violent. To make matters worse, the bottom had fallen out of the watch business by the end of 2003. I was virtually giving my stock away as security against my loans.

Then I borrowed another £150,000 from an Essex jeweller. He knew a lot of criminal faces, so, as usual, I was risking life and limb by borrowing yet more money.

I even owed £400,000 to my suppliers in Hatton Garden but somehow I managed to borrow enough money to pay this back. God knows how I did it, but it involved yet more loans from sharks. My so-called friend Lee's brother was another lender. He had a bad credit rating and so he bought a load of watches through me and then I had to make the monthly payments to pay back a debt of his. I even put a car he owned through my own books as a favour.

Yet, in the middle of all this financial chaos, I still had a dreadful weakness for cars. Besides the brand-new BMW 320 convertible, which I'd given to my secretary, there was a £100,000 Merc SL in my name plus a Bentley Turbo which I bought with my dad, as well as a brand-new Range Rover which cost £65,000. And then there was the brand-new Porsche worth £70,000 and a Mini worth £14,000. And guess what – they were all paid for out of finance loans.

My dad was mystified as to where I was getting all my money from, although he had worked out a long time ago there was a massive storm brewing. On several occasions, he tried to talk to me about my finances but I just reassured him all was fine. Yet again, it was a massive error on my part, as he only wanted to help. In July 2003, we were about to go on another holiday and I went to my parents' house and parked my Porsche in their driveway so they could keep an eye on it and the bailiffs wouldn't find it.

Mr Big and the rest of the Indians were talking about killing me by this stage. They were openly promising to shoot me and then chop me up. But I reckoned the only good thing about owing them so much money was that they didn't really want anything bad to happen to me otherwise they wouldn't get their cash. Ironically, owing them money was helping keep me alive.

I knew I was in deep trouble so I drafted in criminal Den again as I knew he'd protect me, and because he also wanted the money that was owed to him. He was a tough character who openly admitted having problems with some of the biggest names in British crime. But he seemed to have their respect so I knew he was the key to my survival.

One day, Den was in my office when two black Mercs turned up containing six heavies, including a guy called Fisher from west London. Den immediately went outside and talked to them and then we tried to broker a deal to keep the heat off me for the moment.

We eventually retired to a restaurant and I even had my heavyweight muscle man/minder Ali in the background making sure my back was covered; John was the minder for Mr Big and he had come to warn me not to fuck around. He earned a small fortune keeping Mr Big alive, and now it was Den's time to start doing the same for me.

9

LUCKED OUT

1 April 2003 was a typical day for all sorts of very worrying reasons.

The day before, I'd gone back to my house in Chigwell as the removal men were packing up all our belongings because we had sold the house. I felt sick to the core to be leaving Chigwell; I was really depressed about it. I really thought I would stay in Chigwell for the rest of my life, but Nic's friends had all left for north London so the time seemed right for us to go. I was also well aware of my mounting problems with Essex, so I did not try to stop the move.

Then, as the boxes were being loaded into the lorry, my mortgage broker called to say we were £130,000 short to complete on the house. I immediately made a lot of phone calls and managed, miraculously, to borrow the amount off my old friend Jonathan Dennis. It was very tricky explaining to him what had happened because it made me sound like a bad loan risk to put it mildly, although this was the broker's total cock-up.

Jonathan had lent me money in the past but luckily I had always paid him back; I knew, though, that I had to offer him interest, otherwise he would not be happy to oblige. I told him about what had happened and made out I had loads of watches to sell. So he lent me the money.

I was in a real panic that day because Jonathan said the money would take a few days to come over. So we had to organise money transfers to make sure it arrived in time for the completion of the house purchase. I was still hiding everything from Nic and the pressure was really getting to me. I had the removal van literally packing up the house, while there was still a real danger I might not be able to afford the new property.

Our new house was costing a million borrowed pounds. It had six bedrooms and was in a gated community. I even had a double garage for my cars. But it was all a façade, even though I still thought it would all be OK in the end and I'd talk my way out of this mess.

Jonathan's money got through and we ended up in the new house, thank goodness. That first night in bed, it smelled so nice to be in a property that was brand new. My wife was so happy but, as ever, she had no idea what was really going on. Then, three or four days later, we went up to Scotland for my father-in-law's 70th birthday party. I wasn't looking forward to it because I owed him and my brother-in-law Barry some money as well. What a surprise.

A few years earlier, my father-in-law said his wife had ten grand and asked me to invest it for her and she'd made two grand in two months. So he then gave me £250,000 for a few months and told me to make him some money with it. I had to pay him £15,000 interest on it, but he had no idea I was using it to pay off other loans. Every month, I paid them interest out of other loans. It was, as ever, sheer madness.

Then Barry found out that our father-in-law had made good money with me and he wanted a slice of the pie, so he lent me £70,000 just before we moved house as well, so I owed him back the money just before that trip to Scotland. I'd done a sneaky thing and put a cheque in his bank account, knowing that it wouldn't clear before we went away. So he'd then think I had paid him back when, of course, I hadn't. That was a classic trick of mine.

Me, Nic, Arabella (then three years old) and Jake (who was one) all flew up to Scotland on British Airways. I was treading on eggshells by this time because I didn't get on well with Nic's family.

Then, on the Monday morning of that trip, my brother-in-law Barry rang his bank and found out the money wasn't in the account. He went berserk at me. I told him to back off. It was more pressure and it was doing my head in, and I was also still trying to hide my financial mess from Nic, which added even more to my stressed state. It was a very tense flight home.

Barry wanted me to go straight to the bank with him, but, of course, I never liked doing that because I had too much to hide. It was a nightmare.

When we got to London, I almost ran away from them at Arrivals to avoid being dragged into the bank. And I was living in a house I couldn't afford. I had to pay my friend Jonathan back immediately and I had at least a hundred grand's worth of interest to pay to a bunch of hoods.

In many ways, it's worse to borrow from people who are 'normal' because they put more pressure on you. At least with gangsters, although you know that you have that immediate threat of being shot, in some ways I prefer it because it's non-personal. To them, it's just 'business'.

On reflection, I should have had over the banks and the straight people a lot more than I did. But the reason I didn't was because I thought I'd escape the mountain of debt eventually if I just kept ducking and diving. I really did believe I would clear it all up. My brother-in-law Barry got back his £150,000 and I paid him interest of £70,000 on top of that but, of course, I only managed that by borrowing yet more money.

September 2003 was Jewish New Year but that didn't stop the heavyweights who were on my tail. They didn't care about my religious priorities. And I don't wear a beard and a hat so I don't exactly look as if I am 'of the faith' in a traditional sense.

Then I had another stroke of the most twisted form of good fortune when I met yet another Essex villain called Rog, who'd initially contacted me because he wanted some watches and jewellery for his wife. Rog was a heavy hitter in the underworld, although I didn't realise it at the time. He was about 60 and went about things in rather a slow way but he had a definite sparkle in his eye and his wife looked and sounded like Peggy Mitchell off *EastEnders*. She was the salt of the earth – a glitzy, old blonde with lots of shoulder pads and dear old Rog idolised her.

Rog came to see me one time about altering a pair of earrings. Rog was very impressed by the pictures of the famous people up on the pristine, white walls of my office and the nice sanded floors, and ended up lending me about £150,000 in cash. I was *that* persuasive back then. My office cost me £600 a month from Lee. It had a really retro feel to it and it worked well for me because it always gave the impression to the lenders that I had money coming in to pay them.

Every now and again, Lee would pop back to England from his hideout abroad and he actually spotted Rog coming out of my office that first time he visited. Minutes after he'd left, Lee was on my case asking what a dangerous old criminal like Rog was doing in my office. I lied and said I supplied jewellery to him.

I eventually went up to his penthouse to discuss the money he'd promised to lend me. I assured Rog it was an 'in-and-out deal' rather than a long-term one but, of course, I was lying through my teeth.

Rog said he was up for it. 'Yeah. I'll have some of that.'

Rog had a classic villain's storage place out in an east London warehouse, and I went up there on my own in the Porsche to get the money from him. He actually handed it to me in a shoebox. It was a bit surreal and I knew I was standing there in a dodgy, empty warehouse and anything could happen. But Rog seemed calm so I was fine. However, you're always thinking in the back of your mind that something might kick off.

Rog was in the company of a few other rather unpleasant-looking people and I was seriously worried that there might be someone there I already owed money to. That was one of my biggest fears back then, because I was fucked if someone else I had fleeced was there. All Rog's mates turned out to have squashed noses and were from Essex. Surprise, surprise. He also had some guys from Holland there for a meeting. Rog owned a storage unit as well and that was where he eventually produced the money in the shoebox. It was a £20-a-day lock-up storage unit similar to the sort of thing many people store their furniture in. It was clever in a sense because no one would have guessed what was going on if they stumbled into the building.

This storage room doubled as his office and Rog simply handed over the shoebox containing £100,000. It included a lot of Scottish money but that was still legal tender down here. I found out later he gave me a load of it because criminals don't like it as they think it's easier to trace. I banked it immediately so I didn't care. The bank asked me about it but I said I'd just done a deal in Scotland. I didn't care about doing that. I always said all this money was loans and I called it that. It was a loan account. Simple as that.

I was due to pay Rog back a week later, so I drove back to see him the following week at his penthouse and said I'd rather give him the whole lot back in one go and not just the interest.

It was a massive gamble because obviously I didn't have any of the money at all. I told Rog I had another deal, so he'd let me roll it out for another couple of weeks. I even took a gamble and offered to pay him his interest there and then, which I did. He was delighted and gave me another £100,000 on the spot. What a result. I now had £200,000 of his money. But, as usual, I was taking a hell of a risk because Rog was a deadly villain in every sense of the word. I put that latest £100,000 in the bank as well.

Then I started mucking him around about his interest. I was late paying him and I fobbed him off for about a week. We were now in September in the middle of Jewish New Year and I invited my mum and dad to stay at our new, six-bedroom house.

We all went to Mill Hill Synagogue together but that night I got a message on my answering machine: 'Hello, Jay ... it's Rog. You fuckin' cunt. Where's my fuckin' money? I'll fuckin' do you, you fuckin no-good cunt.'

'Shit!' I thought.

Not surprisingly, I got into a bit of a cold sweat. I had this special way of leaving messages on people's answerphones without the phone ringing so it went straight to voicemail. So I left a message saying, 'I am really sorry, Rog ...' and made up a story.

I can't remember exactly what it was, but it came out of my 'store' of tall tales, which got a lot of usage at this time. I think I said I got let down badly or something like that. I also mentioned the Jewish holiday and said the person who let me down was very religious and I couldn't get hold of them until Tuesday. 'But don't worry. It will be sorted out soon.' That was it.

I never heard back from Rog until a few days later when I promised him I'd give him interest of £20,000 to make up for the delays.

'Listen, Jay. I never have a problem if you tell me the truth and I'll be happy,' he said.

Now you are probably wondering why I said I had had a stroke of luck. It was luck in its blackest form; you have to remember that, although Rog was a hardened, old-school gangster, to me he had always been as good as gold and he only turned funny with me when I started mucking him around by being late with my payments. I had agreed the interest rates with Rog due to the desperate state I was in; at the time, had someone offered me money at 10 per cent a day, I would probably have agreed to it, that's how mad my life had become. However, two days after giving him that £20,000, tragically Rog had a major stroke. I didn't know any of this until one of Rog's mates, who'd bought jewellery from me, came to see me to say that Rog was seriously ill and unlikely to survive.

Obviously, in the back of my mind, I was thinking, 'Fuckin' hell … I won't have to pay it all back.' But then I thought it had to come out that I owed him all this money because it always does, surely? I even avoided going to the funeral because I knew there would be people there who'd simply want me to pay up and I didn't have money for them.

Then a few days after the funeral, I asked to see Rog's wife because there was some jewellery I'd had remade for him and I thought I should take it back to her. She asked me up to the penthouse flat, and I agreed to meet her there, even though I was taking quite a considerable risk by doing so.

Well, when I got there, she even asked me if there was any money owed on the jewellery and I said, 'No, it's paid for.'

Then a few days after that, I called one of Rog's best mates to explain that I owed Rog money; it was better coming from me than trying to get away without paying. I was shitting myself by this stage. Now I knew it would have to be paid back, but this time it was different – at least with Rog I had known where I stood.

I then had this meeting in Buckhurst Hill with a couple of old-school villains about the Rog money. One of them was very well spoken and didn't seem like a criminal but I found out afterwards he was a renowned 'face', who lived in Marbella, Spain. Both these blokes ended up being a little bit aggressive towards me in their tone. They were very suntanned and it didn't look like fake tan either.

When I'd first walked in, one of them said, 'I suppose you thought you would get away with not paying Rog's money.'

'No, not at all … In fact, it was me that made contact with Rog's best friend …' and I told them that I'd returned the jewellery to Rog's missus.

I knew it was only a matter of time, but I decided to take a real punt and told them that Rog had done a deal with me until January the following year to keep it. They just said, 'OK, fair enough.'

I then offered them the interest that I owed and I told them the deal and they said all right, I could keep the money until January. I said I was going away and I'd be back on 11 January and then I'd come and see them. It all ended up quite amicable. Mind you, by this time, I had paid back £120,000 in interest.

Meanwhile, I was back juggling with money-lenders Den and Lee. I was paying Den £15,000 a month in interest on a £150,000 loan. The trouble is, when you are desperate, you agree to anything. I wasn't even vaguely capable of servicing these debts.

The first thing I did with the £150,000 from Mark was pay off part of my debt to Lee and pay off the watch stock because the watches were funding the interest to a certain degree. Every time I sold a watch, I tried to pay off bits of interest, but to call it an uphill struggle would have been a gross understatement.

Den was living in Marbella and he was happy because I had up to £450,000 of his money and I was due to pay him £45,000 a month in interest. But now I needed another person and that's where Mark came back into the frame. He'd been the one who started me off on this awful, destructive path lending me my first big hit of cash. Within a few months, I owed Mark £1 million in new debts.

Lee suggested I should buy some shares and make a quick killing to get out of the shit. But then he went and disappeared on me completely, which was good in one sense because I didn't have to pay him any money back for a while, but it was scary in another way because he had been watching my back for me.

Here's a typical outline of my week's debts. They had shrunk a bit but they were still frightening: £45,000 a month to Den; £9,000 a month to Lee; £60,000 a month to Mark; £40,000 a month to Mike West; £20,000 a month to Ali; £25,000 a month to Grant; and around £10,000 a month reducing the deficit to Jonathan and Lucas. That's close to £200,000 in interest alone towards the end of 2003.

And, of course, the villains all thought I still had money coming in, which was absolute bollocks. There was no way I could generate the money to pay off those interest payments. The only way was to keep borrowing money. But, in reality, the only way to survive properly was to try to start paying off the actual loans. But I had absolutely no idea how I was going to do that.

Oh, I almost forgot – I had also borrowed £75,000 off a guy from Manchester on 10 per cent. And then there was another character who I had borrowed £470,000 from. Where would it all end?

That deal with the bloke from Manchester was done on a strictly short-term basis. I was going to give him £50,000–£60,000 interest on the £470,000 but for a period of three to four weeks maximum. But this guy wasn't a criminal and he drove me mad because he didn't appreciate the 'rules' like the underworld did. And, throughout all this, people were still coming to my house and spotting the Porsche and Range Rover and presuming, as ever, that I had more than enough money to pay them all back.

The pressure of funding each debt was appalling. I was waking up every night in a cold sweat, and that was if I even managed to get any sleep. I didn't have the patience to explain it all to my wife. I'd leave her some cash on the kitchen table and hope she wouldn't ask any questions. I wasn't paying off any credit cards any more. I'd just find the next lender and try to use some of that cash to pay off credit cards and the mortgage.

But I still always looked forward to Christmas because I could switch off and have a nice holiday. But this particular Christmas of 2003 I wasn't selling anywhere near enough watches and we were getting closer and closer to a holiday I could clearly ill afford. Then I borrowed half-a-million quid off a guy called Clive on the basis I had to get some watch stock. He charged me 6 per cent a month. It was about £150,000. Then I borrowed more money off him and, by the end of 2003, I owed him half-a-million quid. He then wanted a lump sum of £150,000 even though I was paying his interest and that put me under even more pressure.

But I reckon he must have known I couldn't pay it back. He wrote a cheque out from the NatWest Bank and I put it in my Coutts bank account. I gave him a couple of hundred grand back eventually and, as long as he saw some money, he seemed happy, although I was well aware that we would eventually come to a crunch point when he wanted it all back.

There was another guy called Matt who had a pawnbroking and money-lending business as well as being a dealer in jewellery. He was renowned as a fighter rather than a talker. I borrowed £270,000 off him to fund all the interest I owed; there was just no stopping it. Why couldn't I see it for what it really was? But I was way beyond being able to take stock, and try to turn things around sensibly – I'd long since thrown caution to the wind.

What you have to understand is that, while all this was going on, I was getting more and more behind in paying the interest that I owed. The result was phone calls that would make your heart stop, such as the one I got from criminal Den White, now based in Marbella, who said, 'If I don't get fuckin' paid in the next 48 hours, I am going to fuckin' get on the airplane and come to England and fuckin' wrap your bollocks around your head, you fuckin' cunt. Sort it out!' And these were the guys who were supposed to be on my side!

Clive was piling on the pressure about that £500,000 loan and would often call the house. Thank goodness Nic never had a clue what he was referring to. I made out to her that Clive was nagging me for a watch. Then there was Mr Big still claiming I owed him £700,000 from that VAT deal connected to the diamonds. I was starting to feel like that Henry Hill character in *GoodFellas* who knows everyone is after him and starts to get incredibly paranoid. But at least he was an out-and-out criminal and knew perfectly well what the risks were. I was nothing more than an ordinary Joe who'd started borrowing money off the wrong sort of people. I couldn't even be bothered to deal with the Indians by that stage. I was getting close to not really caring any more, which meant I would be prone to making mistakes.

Yet, bizarrely, there was still something highly satisfying about actually managing to pay off a debt occasionally. I'd call Mark for example, and say, 'Mark, I have your dough.' It was such a relief to be able to say those words. Ironically, half the time they didn't believe me but, of course, there was always someone else lurking around for more money, so my happiness would always be short-lived.

10

BORROWED TIME

It was very hard for Nic because she sensed the chilling undercurrent of what was going on but had no idea of the actual daily threats to my life and the physical abuse. All she saw with her own eyes was me coming home with £50,000–£100,000 in cash in my hand and peeling off £5,000 for her 'shopping money'. In some ways, I'd presumed she knew what was going on but that was simply my way of dealing with it. How on earth could she know I was in debt for millions when we had £150,000 worth of cars in the driveway? Yet I'd go nuts with her for overspending. I was all over the place. Poor Nic. I thought it was easier to let her carry on shopping than tell her the truth. What a stupid mistake that was.

And I was so on edge that it inevitably ended in tears sometimes. One night, just before the Christmas holiday of 2003,

Nic and I were about to go out and Nic walked down the stairs in a very tight-fitting, brief outfit that looked a bit tarty in my opinion and I told her so. Naturally, she exploded at me. I then went off on one and called her a selfish bitch and started telling her she didn't know how much pressure I was under.

I begged Nic to stop spending so much money, but then the credit card bills would turn up and I'd see she had still ignored me and continued to spend massive amounts. It was all adding to the pressure that was building inside me. On one occasion, I found she'd put down a £1,000 deposit on a dining-room table after I told her to stop spending money.

My father-in-law had obviously worked out what was happening and yet he didn't mention anything to his daughter. I got a call from him at 7.00am one morning after he'd found out from my brother-in-law Barry that I had borrowed more money and he sensed I had big problems and was worried he might lose some of the money he'd also lent me.

'What's going on, Jay? Have you lost my money?'

I tried to calm him down, and I gave him all his money back soon after that plus £125,000 in interest. He then had a break from lending me anything for about three or four months, but then he came back in with £150,000. I returned him £75,000 of that money and that's where we are today.

Criminal Terry – whom I knew from the days when I worked in that small jewellery shop in Chigwell – also came back on the scene. He was old East End with a strong accent. I never felt comfortable around him and I hated the way he spoke to his wife in front of me. The real crims thought he was a two-faced coward but I formed my own opinion of him. He'd gone to prison in August 2002 and, while he was in prison, Terry's daughter had fallen off an apartment balcony and been seriously injured. I'd been there at the time and was the first one on the scene to try to help, so in a sense he owed me for coming to her rescue and making sure she got the right medical attention.

Terry didn't seem very grateful for what I had done for his daughter. Then, weirdly, right out of the blue, he lent me £50,000 on 5.5 per cent interest but all that did was pay a small amount of the other massive interest repayments I owed. I really was caught in the middle of the ultimate vicious circle.

So I was barely keeping the sharks at bay. On 23 December 2003, I was in the BA lounge at the airport with my family, about to go to Florida on a holiday I didn't have the money to pay for, when I got a call. It was from the very scary Grant and he said he was going to come after me because I was late paying him. Luckily, he didn't know I was in the BA lounge and about to leave the country. I immediately called my secretary and told her to close the office down until the New Year. I didn't want Grant turning up there looking for his money.

We all flew Club class on that holiday, and we even took Hazel, our cleaner, on holiday with us to look after the kids, so Nic and I could have some time together. I would never just pay for Club for myself like some people I knew. If that plane came down, I would not want them in another part of the aircraft. The flights cost £10,000 and the holiday in total about £25,000. I was broke but I still did it. I'd paid for it out of yet another loan from a criminal. If only they'd known.

Then, on Christmas Eve, just after we'd arrived in Florida, Clive called my wife and told her all about my money problems. Nic confronted me and asked me what the hell was going on.

'There's been a bit of aggravation,' I explained. 'I do owe some money but I have money coming back to me, so let's have a good holiday and worry about it when we get back.'

Obviously, I remained very tight-lipped about it. I had my precious AmEx card and just maxed it out on the holiday. Luckily, Nic rarely looked at the credit card statements.

The holiday went fine for a couple of days but I obviously had a lot on my mind and my wife was now starting to really press me about our financial situation after that call from Clive. I tried to bury myself in the kids and give them a nice time because they deserved it, but my mind was elsewhere. I was really running scared.

I don't think I truly realised how much shit I was in. I never once sat down with a pen and paper and wrote down the figures but at this point I owed a staggering £7 million. It was complete and utter madness. I just kept avoiding the obvious issues. I knew it was too much money and I was frightened to face the reality of what I had done.

Meanwhile, my dad was being drawn further into my problems. The previous Sunday, he'd had a knock on his door from one of my main money-lenders, Mark, although it wasn't anything too heavy. Far from it; Mark broke down and started crying in front of my dad and saying, 'I've lost everything. What am I going to do?' It turned out that all the money I owed Mark had come from a much heavier villain who was now threatening to kill Mark if he didn't pay him back. Talk about a cycle of fear.

My dad is such a nice guy that he told Mark not to worry and was about to wave goodbye to him when, in the middle of all that, Terry also turned up at my dad's house.

My dad was understandably very worried and rang Lee, who came and calmed down both men. Terry had been so furious he'd threatened to drive off the brand-new Range Rover that was parked outside my dad's house. Little did he know that it belonged to Mark, so that wouldn't have helped much!

So now my poor dad had been dragged into my terrible mess of a life. Over the space of a few days, both my dad and wife now knew what was happening. I was relieved in a sense, but it was wrong to involve them and I knew that in my heart of hearts.

My dad was incredible. He immediately told me he was going to try to do some deals with the gangsters to get the high cost of my loans down.

'But why the fuck do that, Dad? I haven't got any money to pay them with,' I told him on the phone. 'You're just going to make things worse.'

My dad was only trying to help save his stupid son's skin so my response must sound a bit harsh, but my dad just didn't appreciate how dangerous some of these characters really were.

Not surprisingly, none of these criminal money-lenders would give Dad a figure and I eventually had to tell him, 'You're not helping, Dad,' and got him to step back and let me try to sort out my own mess.

Back in Florida on New Year's Eve, Nicole and I had been invited to Alan Sugar's mansion in Boca Raton that evening. The kids stayed at the hotel with Hazel. I felt very awkward about seeing the Sugars because I was a broken man and they had no idea what had been happening to me. At one point during the evening, I felt like dropping to my knees and begging Alan for help, but I kept up the old pals act and did my best 'good old Jay' routine.

But once we had got through New Year's Eve, I had to face the reality that I was living on borrowed time. Another couple of days and everything would come crashing down.

I even went to see my parents' oldest friend, Cyril Dennis, at his home near Alan's, in Boca. At first, I had to make mundane conversation with his wife and mother until he turned up. Then I plucked up the courage to ask Cyril if I could talk to him alone and we both went off to his study. It was a huge room in a massive house and quite intimidating. It felt like walking in to see the President of the USA in the Oval Office at the White House. I was very nervous.

So I stood with this man who had known me most of my life and I poured out my story and told him how I had fucked up my life beyond belief. I didn't tell him the full story but he soon got the message that I was deep in the shit. All he said when I left the house was not to worry and that 'we' would sort it all out. I had no reason to disbelieve him because I had seen him help so many other people in our community before.

I then went to visit Alan at the Sugar mansion a few hours before we flew back to the UK. The night before the meeting, I got very stressed and shaky. I found it impossible to sleep; I tossed and turned for about four or five hours after the kids and Nic had dropped off, and finally I walked out on to the balcony of the hotel and thought about killing myself. I stood there for ages. Surely it had to be easier to jump than face the killers and thieves awaiting me back in the UK?

My entire family was so innocent of what was happening. None of it was their fault. We were just a normal family on holiday. I'd even started to explain a few things to Nic early that night and, after telling her what was happening, I'd still felt optimistic. But that was always my problem – I'd keep my head buried in the sand until it was too late.

Knowing I was going to see Alan Sugar at his mansion didn't make things feel any better, either. I knew it was a hopeless move. Typically, I'd told Nic that everything would be all right when it was far from good. I knew Alan Sugar would be quite harsh with me. He always was. He rarely showed his sentimental side, and why should he, anyway? I had got myself into this mess, so he'd quite rightly point out that the only course of action was for me to return to the UK and face up to my responsibilities. Unfortunately for me, those 'responsibilities' included dealing with criminals who'd stop at nothing to get what they were owed, plus interest.

I was getting closer and closer to jumping off that balcony when Jake's voice snapped me out of it. I turned away from my flirtation with ending it all, and got him a drink. The moment had passed. I shook off the feeling of guilt, at contemplating the destruction of my family through my selfishness, and fell into a fitful sleep.

I'd gone to see Alan Sugar for a chat about a business proposition. In truth, I was hoping he might help bail me out of my troubles but I simply did not have the guts to ask him outright for help. Ironically, he seemed quite interested in my idea to sell air space for his company called Amsair and we agreed to talk about it more in London. It was a farce. I had gone in there hoping I could switch the conversation round to my dire circumstances, but I didn't have the bottle.

After I left, he heard on the grapevine that I was in financial trouble and phoned me at my hotel and asked me to come and see him a second time. I was so relieved when I got his message on my voicemail. And I dared to hope that the fact he wanted to see me meant he was going to help me.

So, at 9.00am, I went back to his house and he immediately treated me differently. There was none of the old pals act from the previous day. Alan actually took a fairly firm stance with me because he just could not get his head round how much financial trouble I was in. He told me what a fool I had been to my family but, after a few minutes, he calmed down and started to give me some more friendly advice about how to cope. He told me to negotiate with my creditors, but then I pointed out that, without any funds, I had nothing to negotiate.

Alan Sugar looked at me in horror because it was finally dawning on him that I wanted him to bail me out financially. He made it crystal clear that he was not going to help and even told me that I must have been mad for thinking him or Cyril would help me. Looking back on it, I suppose I was grateful he didn't bullshit me.

But, incredibly, I got the backing of Cyril Dennis that same day, despite Alan Sugar's assertion that no one would help me. Cyril said he'd stump up £1 million for me to negotiate with.

So, a few hours later, on 10 January 2004, I was on that BA flight back to London from the holiday in Florida. I was sitting on the plane thinking about my desperate situation, convinced that no money would ever really materialise.

We eventually arrived home early on Saturday morning to be greeted by my mum and dad. The atmosphere was dreadful. It felt like someone had died. It was made even worse when my mum told me that Mike West, the car dealer, had called. I asked my mum if she had told him I was going to be home and, of course, she had told him, which, in effect, meant that the entire underworld now knew I was back to face the music. Not good news.

It was ironic, really, because my mum had thought she was helping me. Naturally, the panic started to set in virtually the moment I got home. My mate Jamie then came round and he tried to convince me to go and confront them all. Jamie wasn't afraid of anyone; he wanted me to tell them all to fuck off, which probably wouldn't have been such a bad idea but I was too scared to do it.

As the day progressed, I had to start dealing with the practical side of my situation. I had to explain to our maid that I could no longer pay her wages, so she left there and then and we were meant to collect the dog from the kennels but I didn't have the £200 we owed them. So we sat there and waited for the £1 million I prayed that Cyril Dennis would lend me to get me out of this mess. Talk about desperate. I think I knew deep inside that that million would never show up, but I had to believe in something.

One minute we were up and talking about the money turning up and the next moment we were in the depths of despair. My friend Jamie couldn't understand why Nic's wealthy parents wouldn't help us out, but I wasn't surprised by that. Nic even went to see them to make one last desperate appeal, but I knew it was hopeless.

Jamie convinced Nic to go and see her parents. Nic really knew it would be a waste of time but felt she had no choice. My secretary drove her there. They approached the big, black, electric gates and drove to the front door, and were greeted by the huge German shepherds that were always running around the grounds. Nic's dad had a firearms licence and he was sitting in the kitchen with a gun on the table. He really believed gangsters were going to come for him. That's how crazy the whole thing had become.

Nic's father made it very clear there was no way he was going to help as things stood. He added that he'd help on one condition – if she left me. When Nic returned, she was a broken woman; she just could not believe how callous her parents had been, although, in their defence, I guess they must have had their reasons.

I didn't really know what to do. I'd come back to London thinking I might get that loan and now I was back at square one.

That night, Jamie and my secretary both stayed at my house with my parents and Nicole and me. Things had got so heavy while I was away that there were genuine fears something might happen, and they were there in case I had any problems. There was a feeling that none of the real psychos would try to take a pop at me when so many family members were present. My dad just didn't know what to do. He wanted me to go to the police but I knew that no one had actually done anything to me yet, so why would the police be interested? I was just a reckless guy who'd got himself into a really sticky situation. But it was all my fault.

I would never be able to explain in words how broken my mother was. The guilt I have on a daily basis is something that will remain with me for the rest of my life. My mother was finding it impossible to cope, and I was solely responsible. She did not deserve to be going through what I had done to her, and it was particularly painful for me when I knew that she had done everything possible to give me the best upbringing anyone could ever have had. She'd literally have thrown herself in front of a moving train for me and my sister and now I had single-handedly destroyed everything she had worked so hard to achieve for her family.

That Saturday night was by far the worst moment of my life.

11

YOU CAN RUN ...

At 7.30 the following morning, my mum and dad went back to their house in Chigwell after staying the night with me. Nothing had happened at my house after all. Jamie went home quite early. I rang a good friend I had known for most of my life, and in fact she had been staying in the same hotel in Florida with her family. I told her what was going on; she was in so much shock but she took our kids off our hands.

We'd been away for two weeks but all the villains I owed money to started calling each other and word was out that I was back. Trust me, my return was spreading like wildfire. After everyone had left the house, it was just Nic and me at home. Poor thing, she tried to make herself busy around the house in order to act 'normal'.

Nic and I didn't really know what to do, so I then made a list of all the potential friends who could lend me money. There was

Dennis who had to be good for fifty grand; my mate Simon should be able to cough up fifty grand, and so it went on and on. Looking back on it, it was pathetic. I came up with a list of so-called potential lenders and it got to £1 million, so now all I had to do was call them all and get them to give me the money. Obviously, much easier said than done.

I tried to avoid telling them all how much I owed to other people because £1 million was nothing compared to the £7 million I was in hock. I just needed enough money to pay the interest to buy myself some more time, although this would have been eventual suicide as I was locked into a never-ending spiral of mounting interest payments, which I was now unable to service.

I had £400,000 equity in my house but I was trying to avoid throwing that into the mix. In any case, £400,000 would only have been a drop in the ocean by this stage.

A few close mates came round and were in shock about what was happening but at least I was being honest about it now, which was a relief in many ways. But most of our friends and family just couldn't get their heads around the figures and the threats to me; it was alien to most of them. This was a world they had nothing to do with.

I told Nic that morning, 'You have to go back to America.'

She said she had nowhere to stay so I got my dad to ring Alan Sugar and ask him for help again on the phone, but he said there was no way he was going to lend me any money. Then I spoke to Alan's wife Ann and asked her, if I sent Nic back to America, if they would let her stay in their house. She insisted I spoke to Alan first but he was less than enthusiastic, saying, 'Why can't she stay at her sister's?'

I pointed out that Nic's sister didn't have any beds and Alan kindly sent money to buy some. It was all desperate stuff. Then Nic announced she didn't want to go to America on her own.

We got to Sunday night and realised we couldn't stay at the house and then I heard from this guy called Marty, one of Nic's oldest friends, to whom I'd owed £150,000. We had been working together for a couple of years, and in that time I had introduced him to some of my contacts and he made money with them through stocks and shares. I had already paid him a massive amount of interest, but I still owed him money. In truth, he could have called it quits after the fortune he had made on the back of the contacts I'd given him, but maybe I'm just being naïve.

To give him his due, he kindly picked us up from our house that night and drove us to the airport. I'd turned my phone off because I couldn't face the barrage of abusive calls; I used a pay-as-you-go mobile instead. At the airport, Marty dropped us off and he assured me that everything would be all right and we would get everything sorted. If he had been a criminal, he would never have been so calm about the money I owed him and I have a lot to thank him for.

I then spoke to my friend Lucas, who dropped everything he was doing and ran to my aid. Lucas really tried to help me, even though I owed him a very large amount of money. He was still 100 per cent behind me, and willing to race over to the airport hotel where we were staying. Mind you, there was no avoiding the money I owed him as well.

Lucas paid for Nic and the kids to fly to France the next day to meet her mum in Paris so they could get out of the way of any threats to us, that's how good he was. Eventually, that evening at the airport hotel, Nic went to bed and the kids fell fast asleep.

That night, Lucas asked, 'What the fuck is going on?'

I told him, and he urged me to call our mutual friend Ali, who would protect me for a price.

'Fuck 'em,' he said after I told him about the characters who were after me.

We talked until 2.00am and tried to go through all the debts and how it had all escalated. It was even more scary when you lumped it all together and realised the sheer scale of it all.

Ali the negotiator turned up and pointed out that I owed another heavyweight character called Fisher £450,000, and if I paid that off then I would get the protection from Fisher, which might stop all the others coming after me.

Then I could start working again and Ali said he'd tell everyone I was working with him and that I would repay the other money eventually. He reckoned they would leave me alone, which would give me some breathing space.

At about 7.00 the next morning, I left the airport hotel before Nic because I had things to do; her mum would meet her in Paris. I was trying to kiss Arabella goodbye and I couldn't get her to wake up, and then I started to think she was obviously not meant to wake up and that freaked me out.

Suddenly, I started crying because she wouldn't wake up. It was a horrible moment of panic. Arabella was fine but not being able to wake her made me question my own mortality.

Then I disappeared, not even knowing when, or if, I would ever see them again. Ricky, someone else I owed money to, and a driver came to the hotel and we drove to my office in Romford.

My dad met us there and I gave the keys to the safe to Ricky and said he should take out whatever he wanted. I really was past caring. There were diamonds and watches and he picked up £100,000 worth, which at least would give me some breathing space in relation to his debt.

Then we drove to my dad's factory nearby, where I kept most of the stock, and for the first and only time I saw my dad cry. We were in an office on our own and he just grabbed hold of me and started crying and said, 'They're going to kill you ... they're going to kill you.'

I said, 'No, no, Dad. They won't kill me because I owe them money. We will sort this out. I promise you.'

I still relied on that old chestnut, but for how much longer?

Dad was a bit out of control but you can hardly blame him, can you? He was usually very cool and collected, but he was so out of his depth over what was happening to me. It was all like a bad nightmare. He did manage to straighten himself out very quickly, though.

Then I drove to Lucas's gated mansion in north London. I'd checked to make sure we were not being followed all the way. Lucas's girlfriend was there and she immediately told me to relax.

I was exhausted and very tense. I had jet-lag from Miami and I hadn't slept for three nights. I was fucked.

Lucas's girlfriend made us dinner but then Ali turned on me and accused me of taking the piss. I couldn't handle it and burst into tears. I said I was scared for my kids' lives. Then Ali backed off and tried to make light of it, but I knew we were dealing with some of the heaviest criminals in Britain and, if *he* was angry, then God knew how they felt about me.

I stayed at Lucas's house that night, and the next day he drove me to a hotel close to Hyde Park where Lucas knew the manager, so I could stay there discreetly and they'd keep an eye on me. Lucas had to leave me to go back up the M1 for work. I stayed at the hotel for three days and three nights and saw absolutely no one – not even my family.

I was so tired that I slept most of the time. I didn't call anyone except for Nic from that new pay-as-you-go phone. Then a few days went by and Ali returned and took me under his wing and said once again we had to get that £450,000 to Fisher.

I then had a meeting with Fisher who turned out to be sympathetic; he said I should get a pen and paper and write down all the people to whom I owed interest, and he'd go and see them all, knock down all the interest, get some of the money off them and say it was my money he was taking. Then Fisher stunned me by announcing I actually owed him £1 million, but I was in no position to argue – at least he was going to help me.

I wouldn't agree to see the lenders with Fisher because I

thought it was going to make things worse. At the end of the day, I'd be telling them there wasn't any money and they'd go bananas. They'd be sure to come after me then. I felt I had to be sensible. But Fisher turned it round and said I was the victim and these people were taking the piss. But, of course, he could say anything he wanted – all he cared about was his own money.

But my dad reckoned I should just drip feed Fisher to get the others off my back. Then, without my knowledge, my dad went up to the West End to see some of the straighter characters to whom I owed money. He was determined to get me out of my mess.

Then I got a message to meet my dad and solicitor a few hours later at the hotel where I was staying.

I felt uneasy. I knew he was only trying to help but I felt as if something wasn't quite right. Down in the lobby, it was very quiet and there were two men dressed in suits making a call on the house phone. I heard one of them say, 'We're in reception and we'll see you down here.'

I was immediately suspicious, so I decided to walk out, but, as I was about to go through the revolving doors, one of them came up to me and said, 'Jason Shifrin?'

'Yes.'

'Don't panic. We're police and you've got to come with us.'

With that, a dark-blue people carrier pulled up outside the hotel and they insisted I get into it with them. We drove off almost immediately. For all I knew, they might have been lying and could have been kidnappers about to hold me for ransom.

I started to panic a bit and insisted on seeing their identification. They showed me their warrant cards and said we were on our way to Scotland Yard. It felt completely surreal as we went through the barrier at Scotland Yard. I really did not know what the hell was going on.

Then it finally dawned on me that maybe something had happened to my dad.

'Is my dad all right?' I asked.

'Yeah. We've got your dad. He's fine.'

But then nothing else was said until we got into an interview room at the Yard.

'Right,' I asked them, 'what is going on?'

It was only then they told me that Dad was in a hotel round the corner from Scotland Yard and that he was 'absolutely fine'.

'But what's happened?' I asked.

'We believe you were about to be kidnapped.'

They claimed they'd been told by my solicitor that there was a chance I would be snatched by a gang of criminals. I naturally denied it, telling them, 'That's absolute bullshit.'

In any case, I was more concerned about my dad than any threat to me. I wanted to know how he was, so I tried to explain it all away by saying, 'All that happened was that I was meant to be paying some money to someone tomorrow and there is nothing more to this. No threats ... no danger ... nothing. I don't know what all the fuss is about.'

But then one officer chipped in, 'We know the people you owe money to and we have seen the list of others you owe money to and we will protect you. We will put specialist officers with you. We will record stuff.'

I was horrified. This was the last thing I needed. 'No ... you don't understand,' I said, 'they are just asking for their money back. No one's kidnapped me and no one's threatened me. That's it.'

I told them I was going to be in real trouble if I stayed with them any longer because I was due back at my hotel for a meeting and I didn't have my mobile with me. Then I finally turned the conversation back round to my dad. A detective drove me round to see him and he said he thought I was about to be kidnapped so he'd alerted the police. He was only doing what any anxious parent would do if they heard one of their kids might be in trouble.

I tried to be understanding towards my dad because he'd clearly been very worried about my safety. 'It'll be fine, Dad. They won't snatch me. They need their money more than they need me. I just want to pay them off and have some kind of normal life again.'

My dad looked at me as though I was mad, but it was important for him to know I appreciated his concern, even though it threatened to cause me a lot more problems.

So I then made sure my dad was OK and got back to the hotel at about 1.00am.

The next morning, Ali turned up at about 9.00am and we went in two Range Rovers to a hotel on the outskirts of south London where I was to meet Cyril Dennis's solicitor who was going to hand me the loan he had promised me. The loan was to be to my dad on the back of him giving the Dennis family security on his properties in England and Spain.

But then the terms of the loan changed. I immediately phoned Cyril as I sat there with his solicitor and explained that I had two loan sharks waiting outside for the money and now was not the time to sentence me to instant death. It worked and he paid £400,000. It wasn't the million I was after but it would certainly help.

I arranged for the money from the house transaction to be released as security and the solicitor gave us the banker's draft. I then gave it to Ali and he went off to sort it all out. I continued staying at that hotel on the edge of Hyde Park. I used to walk round the park every morning, and my mum and dad would often come to visit me to try to keep my spirits up.

In January 2004, Nic moved with the kids to a friend's house in Israel even though she was desperate to get back home to England. But we didn't even have a house any more so I couldn't even see how we'd ever be together again as a family. It was a horrible period for us all.

The whole family was in limbo and it was all my fault. So many of my friendships had been put to the test by my borrowing. And I couldn't even use my old phone any more so no one could get in touch with me.

I went into a terrible pit of depression. On Valentine's night in February, the hotel where I was still staying had a huge function. But I was in my room all on my own with nowhere to turn. I couldn't go in the bar of the hotel in case I was spotted; I couldn't eat in the restaurant for the same reason. I was completely trapped. Even when I went through reception, I used to go through with a robber's woolly hat on as a disguise. It was a desperate existence.

Anyone could have spotted me. The day following Valentine's Day, I got in the lift and there was someone in there whom I recognised. I was so freaked out I hid myself from him. Back in my room, I put together yet another list of all the people I owed money to, and then Ali picked me up from the hotel one evening and said we should phone them all. I began each call by saying to them I was back in England and I would pay them.

They were all pleased to hear from me because they'd all presumed I'd skipped the country. The only person who wasn't interested in talking to me was Grant. He said, 'Not interested. Not talking to you.' Then he put the phone down on me.

I remember Ali calling that lender Mark and saying in an Irish accent that the IRA were involved with my debt and all that bollocks in a bid to try to make him pull away from me but I knew it wouldn't work. These people were not stupid.

The next big thing that happened was that March. My best man Andrew came back again and said he would lend me the money to rent a house and he very kindly coughed up £6,500. I didn't really deserve it.

I quickly found a very small mews house in central London close to the hotel I had stayed in from January to March. It had cost a small fortune and Lucas paid for it all. It must have been over £5,000 and I still owed him about £150,000 on top of that. What a guy!

The house we rented was in Sussex Gardens, Paddington. Fisher and Ali were insistent I stayed in the west London area so I remained on their patch. They convinced me no one would touch me while I was on their manor.

The £6,500 covered six months' rent and I leased the house under a different name. The good news was that Nic was coming back after agreeing to join me. Ali said they shouldn't come back but I insisted; I couldn't live any longer without them. My family were my only salvation. If I lost them, then nothing would be worth living for.

12

THE SINS OF
THE SON

After a couple of months on my own in that hotel, my hair was long and greasy and I had a beard and I looked terrible. The kids didn't even recognise me and were quite standoffish at first when Nic joined me at the house. She was also quite cold towards me. Not surprisingly, she was confused and had been getting a lot of stick from her family about what I'd done and how she should leave me.

But, once the family all moved in, I started to feel a bit more settled. The house was tiny downstairs and had three bedrooms upstairs.

Thanks to those earlier calls, all my pursuers now knew I was up shit creek and they all seemed to be blaming me for every single debt in London. I had a total of £500 in my pocket but at least the pressure seemed to be off for the moment.

There was nothing I could do, except try to survive. I was still getting 40 or 50 messages a week on my old answerphone but I didn't even check them any more. What was the point?

All the stuff from the other house which had been sold earlier had been packed up by two friends and put in storage. I went and got some of it out of storage and made sure the kids' bedrooms in this new, smaller house were made up to look like their old ones.

My next move was to get in contact with money-lender Den White who had evolved into my protector the previous year. At first, Den was as angry as everyone else with me.

'You cunt … you fucked me over,' he said when I called him up.

I said, 'Den, please, I haven't done anything. Please listen to me. Come and meet me.'

He calmed down and we met up in Notting Hill, west London. I told him I'd been promised by Fisher that I'd be able to go back to work, and my mum and dad had even been paying off some of my debts slowly.

I assured Den I wanted to pay him back and work with him and he said he'd think about it. He wanted £50,000 immediately and, since my mum and dad still had some money in their property in Spain, I gave my word to him that he would get that £50,000 because then I knew he'd be on my side.

But another one of my creditors, Mike West, started telling everyone I'd stolen his money and that I was involved with every criminal in England.

Then even the straight people started to withdraw from me, so

I asked Den to 'have a word' with Mike West and he told him to shut up, otherwise no one would ever get their money back. He agreed because Den is a very persuasive sort of person. Then I dispatched Den to see another heavy hitter, Ali, and he also assured him I'd be sorting out his money soon. Den even visited a couple of my other creditors as well.

At 7.30pm that same night, I got a call from that lender Terry. He wasn't happy and suddenly said, 'Hey, Jase, what's happening round at your mum and dad's house tonight?'

'What do you mean?' I asked.

He then said something must have happened at my parents' house because the police had roped off the street. I'd kept away from the house because everyone was worried I'd be killed or kidnapped or whatever.

I went white in the face and slammed the phone down and called my parents' house immediately. My auntie Hazel answered and then my mum came on the phone.

I said I'd get in a taxi unless she immediately told me what was going on. Finally, she blurted it out: 'Dad's been beaten up.'

'What do you mean?'

'Don't worry. He's OK.'

My dad had been hurt. I was overwhelmed with guilt because it was undoubtedly my fault he'd been targeted. He could have died.

Aunt Hazel then explained how Dad had driven home from work that night after locking up the factory when his staff had left for the day. He had this very familiar, regular routine and somebody must have been watching him because, as he parked his car in the driveway outside his house, two guys in balaclavas jumped out from behind a bush and said they had his wife and he had to go with them.

He agreed but then freaked out when they tried to tape him up because he felt very claustrophobic. Then my dad lashed out at them and so they began kicking and punching him and gave him a right seeing-to.

As my Aunt Hazel told me what had happened, I started to shake because I knew this was all down to me. How could my loving, wonderful parents be dragged into this mess? What sort of a son was I? I didn't deserve them standing by me.

Aunt Hazel then told me how my brave dad scuffled with his attackers and it caused so much noise that my mum was alerted and she immediately dialled 999. The attackers then heard the sirens as police cars approached and ran off.

My dad was incredibly lucky to escape with his life intact, except for a few cuts, bruises and grazes. He was even in reasonable spirits, feeling, rightly, that he was correct to fight back because it stopped them kidnapping him or my mum.

Naturally, the police took it all very seriously and insisted my mum and dad left their house immediately. Their main neighbour was from a well-known Greek family and I'm convinced none of this would have happened if he had been around because he is the sort of bloke no one would dare take on.

Ironically, the other neighbour was in the police force. Not that that made much difference. Anyway, Mum and Dad ended up spending the night in a hotel in Buckhurst Hill.

The following evening, I insisted they stayed in the Royal Lancaster hotel for the night and the following day they moved into our tiny, rented mews house. It was a tight squeeze and they shared a room with Arabella, but it was better than risking any more encounters with the villains who were after me.

I knew I had to take full responsibility for what had happened. It was a measure of how serious things had become. I'd spent too long thinking I could get away with it all and convinced myself it would never really affect my family. The attack on my dad really brought it all home.

It wasn't easy all being cooped up together in that small house but at least we were under the same roof and that felt a lot safer than being apart. My dad insisted he didn't want to pay any more money out to the lenders.

The attempted kidnap had hardened his resolve, which is a credit to his character. He didn't like being pushed around. We could have just handed the family flat in Spain over to Den White to get him off our backs but that would have pissed Cyril Dennis off as he had loaned the money against the flat.

There were a lot of arguments between us as to what to do next. I still felt awful about my dad because he was literally stuck in the middle of it all. He was an honest, hard-working man and the behaviour of these criminals was beyond his comprehension.

Detectives insisted on installing panic buttons in all my families' homes, including my sister, my cousins and my grandmother. They also hid recording material inside the house in case anyone came back. The police wanted to interview me but I didn't even want them knowing where we lived because I knew a lot of criminals had contacts in the force and they'd soon find out where I was.

Eventually – after some heavy pressure from detectives – I agreed to an interview at a police station in Trafalgar Square. One of the officers, a woman, immediately annoyed me by saying my family were blaming me for what had happened.

My mood wasn't helped by the fact I'd also got a barrage of texts that day from the people who'd beaten up my dad. One delightful message read: 'We have your dad's Jewish pig blood all over us.' It was nasty and racist, and it added to my feeling of hopelessness.

Then I got more abusive texts from another lot saying that, now I had got Den involved as my protector, they would give me a six-month extension to repay it all. But I didn't even know who 'they' were. I was literally in debt to a bunch of criminals whose true identity I did not know.

Naturally, I told the police I had no idea who had beaten up my father. It was frustrating but, if I had told them, all it would have done was kick-start the cycle of violence all over again and I was determined never to put my family at risk ever again.

Just as the police interview at Trafalgar Square was coming to an end, two officers I didn't know turned up in the interview room to talk to me about something else. I was then arrested for the theft of watches. I was gobsmacked; I felt like I had been set up.

After cautioning me, the two officers said we were off to Romford nick. I actually suspected it might be a set-up by a bunch of heavyweight criminals and that the moment the cops dropped me off the other end someone would be there to beat me up or maybe even kill me. Just before we left, I was allowed one phone call and managed to get my cousin the solicitor to come and see me at Romford Police Station.

I was pushed into a panda car at Trafalgar Square and I even had to give them directions to Romford from the West End. After four hours in a grim cell, I was pulled in for an interview and thank goodness my solicitor was there. The detectives asked me about certain people's names and then told me some bloke in Manchester had claimed I'd stolen two watches from him.

The truth was that a guy called Billy had given me two watches and was trying to get a false insurance claim going, and, when the police went to my office and found I wasn't there, they just presumed I'd gone on the run. Within a week, all charges were rightly dropped.

A few weeks later, in early April 2004, I was officially made bankrupt. I had to hire four Russian security men to protect me at the county court in case any of my lenders came after me. My uncle Mike – a London cab driver – drove me to pick up the heavies and then he waited outside the court while I attended the creditors' meeting. There were even stories going round that I'd had plastic surgery and that a lot of the lenders would turn up just to see what I looked like in case I tried to make a run for it.

In addition to half of the London and Essex underworld, I also had Lombard, the car finance people, after me for repayments because I never paid off my cars. They had me for £150,000, so I was made bankrupt. Ironically, by this time, all I had was one car worth £700 and a Woolwich Building Society account with £750 in it. I'd given our Mini and the Porsche to my mate Jamie back in January 2004 to dock it off his bill.

At least everybody now knew that I had no money, which wasn't a bad thing after what I'd been through.

Then Marty, the guy who drove Nicole and me to the airport hotel the day after we got back from the US – another of my money-lenders – found a buyer for my house, which had been empty for months. They wanted it with everything in it. The price was £1.1 million and the buyer wanted to pay part of the money into an offshore account; the rest would be on the books, so we agreed it. The offshore would cover the £400,000 I needed to pay off lender Fisher and the other bit of money, which my dad had lent me against his own house.

We stayed in the mews house in Hyde Park until August. My mum and dad sold their house and rented a flat in Stanmore eventually, but half of the money they got for their house had to be paid straight to Cyril Dennis because they'd taken out a loan from him to help me through my problems.

Nic and I eventually rented a house for £1,500 a month in Mill Hill and, of course, I was still getting loads of grief from various characters, who continued chasing me.

By now, everyone knew I was potless but Den was still telling the criminal fraternity that, if they killed me, he'd make sure they got saddled with my debt. The threat of my death was keeping me alive, in a sense.

I tried to step back emotionally but I felt ashamed and upset and disappointed to have caused my wife, parents and family all this trouble. I wanted to repay Dad but my mum kept telling me that my life was far more important to her; material stuff was not important. I am meant to look after my family, not the other way round; it's just how I am made.

It destroyed me in a lot of ways but I still felt I couldn't show it openly. My mum blamed a lot of other people but I tried to take responsibility for my actions. After all, I had caused all this. Yet she was convinced others were to blame.

That guilt was like a prison sentence – I couldn't get away from it. I felt like I had taken my sister's inheritance away from her as well and Nicole's parents were not talking to me and would not give Nicole any financial help unless she left me. Even though I had wrecked Nicole's life, she was like a rock to me, which stopped me from ending my own life, and that's no exaggeration. She was amazing throughout the whole thing, valued family life above anything else and just wanted us to stay as a unit, and it's a shame her parents and sister could not understand that.

In a bid to try to survive, I eventually got myself a job as a car courier delivering parcels all over the south-east. Then I met Lee's brother in town with Ali and we sat down and had lunch.

Then, as we got in Lee's brother's Range Rover, Ali said to me,

'I've got something important to tell you. You have to swear you will not tell anyone.'

'Sure.'

'It was me who done that to your dad. Not me personally, but people I owed money to organised it, but they would never have done it if they had known Den was involved with you. They only found out about him the day after it happened.'

I went cold with rage and at that point I realised how a human could kill another human. I guess he wanted to get it off his chest, and I felt an almost irresistible urge to destroy him for what he'd just told me. You, the reader, will never understand how hard it was for me to stay calm. In a split second, though, I'd decided that it was important to keep your friends close, but your enemies closer.

He explained that he owed people money in Birmingham (which he had given to me) and they said, 'Leave it to us,' and they did it.

By September 2004, I'd managed to chip away at some of the debt to my friend Elliot and Lucas, but I'd only been able to find small amounts. We were so desperate we resorted to selling a lot of our clothes and jewellery on eBay.

Strangely enough, Nicole became a much calmer person after that attack on my father. People everywhere now knew what was going on and used to wonder how Nic could even afford to buy a new dress; eBay was our saviour. I guess a lot of our friends and family also wondered why she stayed with me.

I continued working as a courier for about three months. Meanwhile, my father and mother rarely talked about what had happened and it really bothered Nic that my dad never spoke about it. He had pushed it aside but it was his right to deal with it in any way he wanted. And all through this, I had to put on this hard exterior. I was worried that, if I started crying, I'd never be able to stop.

Everyone was now well aware that a lot of bad people were after me. It was tempting to go to the police but that would have been the end of me so I stuck with my adviser Den in the hope he would continue to protect me. That eventually turned out to be a fatal error, because Den wasn't really helping me at all. Whenever I paid off a debt, Den ended up getting a cash rake-off, so all his motives were questionable. But I still didn't realise that then.

I'd managed to pay off Fisher with my parents' money. He'd been working for Mr Big, who, in turn, owed tens of millions of pounds to just about every villain in Britain. No wonder Fisher was such a nightmare. He was under even more pressure than me because all the money I paid him back went to someone else. What was particularly upsetting later was the fact that I didn't actually owe him anything at all – it just took years for me to realise that.

By the end of 2004, I had Ali, Jamie, Den and Terry all lining up for money I owed them. Meanwhile, I had ended up paying my other remaining creditors more money in interest than they had lent me in the first place.

Then there were a host of other creditors including Mark and Grant, to name but a few. I even managed to talk my dad into giving me another £30,000 for a deal but used it to pay off yet another debt. That was how low I had got. After everything I'd put my dad through, I was still capable of taking him for a ride, but my main priority was to prevent anyone from attacking him again.

Then my so-called mate Den White called me and said the chilling words: 'If I don't get this money back, I will shoot you.' He said it quite nicely – if that's possible! – but the message was clear – I could not keep fucking him around and he'd been my protector up until then. I really was shitting on my own doorstep.

In my eyes, Den was being very unreasonable with me because he reckoned I owed him £400,000, but £250,000 of that was interest, although I have to admit he did stick another £100,000 into my new platinum business. But then I went and used it to pay other people off, which was typically suicidal of me.

Somehow, I talked Den round into being patient and also offered him a share of my loans if he continued to help deal with some of the psychos who were after me. He agreed, but only because he could see it being another earner for him.

13

TUNNEL VISION

In 2005, I started doing some business with my watch-dealer mate Ricky. It was all relatively modest stuff but at least it gave me some kind of *real* income, which was very handy, considering my dire finances.

On one occasion, we were flogging a watch for £20,000 to a buyer, who insisted we meet him near the Dartford Tunnel. I know, I know – it sounds dodgy already, but sometimes a man's gotta do what a man's gotta do.

Anyway, we picked the watch up from a place in Hatton Garden, then I headed with Ricky in my £700 Rover down to the badlands of Kent to a service station just near the entrance to the tunnel. It all felt a bit edgy as this was an area known to criminals as the 'Wild West'.

So Ricky went inside the service area to do the deal. A few moments later, he came out alongside a massive lump of a guy and it looked like there might be a problem. I immediately started to get a bad feeling about the entire deal. Then a horrible thought went through my mind as I studied this huge character lumbering alongside Ricky. He looked really familiar and I realised he was definitely someone connected to my own shady past. But no way was I going to remind him that we knew each other.

Moments later, Ricky came alongside my old banger and introduced me to this bloke. I tried not to look him in the eye in case he remembered me. Then he asked me very politely to take some links out of the watch strap because it was too big or him.

I was so relieved he hadn't worked out who I was I was more than happy to oblige. So I took the watch back, got into the car and began fixing it, while Ricky and this big thug stood next to my Rover. They must have looked bloody suspicious in the middle of that service area because, minutes later, the police rolled up in a car and asked us what we were up to.

I explained to one of the cops that I'd just sold the watch to the 'lump'. It was only then I noticed he had three more 'lumps' waiting for him in his car, which had been parked near us all the time. It looked like a meeting of lower-ranking Mafia bodyguards.

The cop noticed me looking behind him and saw the three other 'lumps'. He immediately called on his radio for back-up. I was soon shitting myself because I knew they'd soon want to know who owned the Rover and I didn't want to say my name in front of this guy because then he'd definitely remember meeting me before and that would be a disaster.

Of course, I was more bothered by the four gangsters than the actual police. Another young copper emerged from a patrol car and appeared alongside me as I sat in the Rover fiddling with the watch strap. He asked me the inevitable question about the ownership of the Rover. I said it was my car and, of course, he then asked me my name, all within earshot of our gigantic buyer.

Then I pulled the young cop aside and lowered my voice before telling him I didn't want the others to know my name. Amazingly, the cop was fine with it and agreed to keep my name quiet. Luckily, my car checked out as a completely legal vehicle. I reckon the police thought I was just selling dodgy watches, but thank God they never even checked the bag that contained the £20,000.

Afterwards, I swore that I'd never allow myself to get into such a tight spot but, of course, I was in a desperate state so I had to go through with any deal that came my way.

In March 2005, my brother-in-law Stefan died tragically of septicaemia, which naturally hit the whole family very hard. I'd spent a lot of time with him during various trips to Miami and, although he'd never actually helped me out with some of my 'cash problems', he had been very good to me in other ways.

The funeral was scheduled to be held in Paris. I knew it was going to be tough because there was a lot of animosity towards me from Nic's side of the family. Her parents had even told Nic that I should not say hello to them at the funeral.

Anyway, we travelled by Eurostar and, within seconds of getting on the train, we bumped into Nic's sister. We quickly broke the ice and soon things were back on a civilised level. Not surprisingly, the actual funeral had a dreadful, sad atmosphere, because my brother-in-law had only been 37.

A couple of days after returning to the UK, we held a birthday party for my son Jake at a local village hall and I made a point of asking Nic's recently bereaved sister to come. But it all ended in tears when my mother-in-law turned up and I was so furious I told her to get out. My friends had to grab hold of me when I lost my temper and smashed the kitchen up.

I only tell these two domestic stories because, in the middle of dealing with psychotic criminals, I was getting deeper and deeper into trouble with my own family. The two pressures seemed to be merging into one. It was awful and it was putting even more pressure on me.

Then, towards the end of 2005, I got a call from a criminal called Eric, whom I'd first met in 2000. He was a bit of a modern-day Arthur Daley with a brand-new Range Rover and pinstripe suits. Eric was raking in £100,000 a week on various dodgy deals and that cash was almost permanently burning a hole in his pocket.

Anyway, I was due to meet Eric in Manchester to sort out a loan on the basis I would cut him in on a watches deal. But I had very bad flu and didn't turn up because I couldn't face the flight up there and I couldn't get hold of him on the phone to tell him the meeting was off. Unfortunately, on the same afternoon that he'd gone to a hotel near Manchester Airport to meet me, he ended up being arrested by 14 Customs and Excise officers.

They also raided his house and office. Eric had £150,000 in cash on him at the hotel, which he was going to lend to me. He told the police it was to buy watches off me. Eric finally got me on the phone and insisted I went up to Manchester to tell the police I'd been due to meet him for completely legitimate reasons.

I felt bad about what had happened to Eric, so I was happy to get on a plane to go and meet him and his solicitor. But first we needed to get our stories straight. He and his brief wanted me to say the money was due to me. But I pointed out that they needed to find a way to say how they got the money in the first place, otherwise the police would never believe their story and just presume it came from drugs or some other criminal enterprise.

So I decided to concoct a story about how my brother-in-law – who'd just died – knew someone up north who could drop the money off at the hotel and that's how Eric came to have it on him. It seemed like a perfect cover story.

A few days later, I went up to Manchester to be interviewed by Customs and Excise in connection with Eric. I took a solicitor with me just for safety's sake. But they arrested me the moment I walked into the police station.

The police then revealed that they were outside my house back in London and they were about to raid it. But they were so badly informed that they were actually waiting outside my sister's house, and I had to explain I did not live there. Then they sent all the cops to my real address after letting me phone my wife to tell her that they were on their way.

My mother-in-law was also at our house at the time but she

left before the police arrived. Nic had to tell the kids that someone was buying the house just before the police arrived to search the premises. It was terrible. While they held me in a cell up in Manchester, a team of cops ransacked the house and took all my computers and everything. Despite being in the house for four hours, they didn't even go in the loft or the shed, which was strange because you'd think they would be the first places they'd look.

Back at the police station, I was eventually interviewed and I told them how my brother-in-law had organised the money in keeping with my pre-agreed story with Eric. I told them I hadn't a clue about the background to the arrangement. And they certainly got a bit of a shock when I added, 'My brother-in-law is dead so I can't ask him any questions about it.'

As the interview continued, I let them know in no uncertain terms that the money I was supposed to have dropped off wasn't my money, and that got me off the hook, thank goodness. Obviously, it must have looked suspicious but they couldn't prove otherwise and I was released without charge.

Meanwhile, my faithful dad kept saying (he even does it to this day) that most of this money I supposedly owed to so many dodgy, dangerous characters wasn't even owed by me really, so everything I was going through shouldn't really have been happening.

Dad always had my best interests at heart but, unfortunately, he didn't really understand that these evil bastards would just keep coming back to harass me more and more. They had me by

Above: The first summer at our house in Chigwell in 1977.

Below left: On holiday in Florida in 1980. I had my moon boots on as we were off to the chillier climes of New York on our way home.

Below right: It was the eighties and the hair was bigger then. With my sister at Mum and Dad's flat in Marbella.

Above: My dad's silver shadow Mark II which he bought in 1983.
I loved that car.

Below: With my grandparents at my wedding in 1998.

Above left: With Daniel Sugar on Alan Sugar's boat, *Louisiana*.

Above right: Alan and Ann Sugar at my wedding in 1998.

Below left: Nicole with our new baby girl, Arabella, in 2000.

Below right: With my son Jacob in Italy in 2003.

Above: These photos were taken when I was in hiding in London. It was heartbreaking being separated from my kids for so long.

Below: With my gorgeous Nicole in December 2009.

the short and curlies. It was nothing to do with right or wrong; in their minds, I'd entered into an 'agreement' with each of them. It didn't matter whether it was fair or not. It really was the law of the jungle out there.

And more incidents kept happening which proved just how dangerous my life had become. After being released by the police, I had hundreds of messages on my phone, including one from a guy called Billy. He was another Essex classic with a flashy new Bentley who loved to party hard. I had borrowed £20,000 from him for a year and was paying him £2,000 a month in interest. So here is this guy who makes £20,000 in interest and yet he was screaming obscenities into my answerphone because I was a few hours late in paying.

Another character, from whom I'd borrowed £50,000, left a message. He'd insisted on taking security to the value of £50,000 so I gave him a load of watches, which he got valued so he was comfortable about the loan. Then, six months later, he thought I had disappeared and wasn't going to pay him so, he claimed, he sold the watches at a ten-grand loss. Then he came after me for the ten-grand shortfall.

I usually tried to pay off the smaller amounts of money to keep the wolves at bay. I even managed to regain the trust of a couple of watch dealers in Hatton Garden, who began letting me buy some watches off them again. Things weren't exactly looking up, but at least I was just about managing to pay the bills.

But, in the middle of all this, one of the main characters I owed money to – Mike West – started to threaten me. He claimed he'd got a bunch of East End villains lined up to kidnap me because of money I owed him. The trouble was that West had a big mouth. He was telling anyone who would listen about my problems, yet he didn't have a clue what was really going on. He was under pressure himself to pay back the money he was lending to me.

It was all about making me sound bad to wind people up to take the 'dairy' (the gangsters' term for the blame). The truth was that West was charging me 10 per cent interest and keeping 9 per cent for himself and paying 1 per cent to the people he was actually borrowing from. But all his bad-mouthing made it even harder for me to get any support from other people, particularly in the local community.

In the end, I had to get heavyweight criminal Den to go round and scare the living daylights out of West again. Den was by now earning good money through me, so he was more than happy to oblige. Den also happened to know West well and had told him in the past to stop bad-mouthing me. But West only took any real notice when Den went round to his office one day and took a photograph of him and 'had words'. It scared the shit out of West.

How could I be so fucking stupid, you must be thinking. Would these sorts of characters really just walk away from someone they could just keep bleeding like me? Of course they wouldn't. But that line between work and family had become so blurred that even my poor innocent sister got pulled into my problems.

'Is Jason there?' a couple of goons asked her one day on her doorstep. Nothing too heavy, just a gentle reminder to let me know that they were still 'thinking about me'.

They didn't know where I was but I had been stupidly using my sister's home as a postal address so they knew I'd get the message they were 'delivering' to my sister's doorstep.

I hated the fact that I was exposing my family to this sort of thing yet again. Obviously, my sister was completely freaked out by the 'visit', although no one was actually hurt or threatened. They were much too subtle for that – at this stage. But I knew the longer my so-called debts kept escalating, the more likely it was that, one day, one of their little 'visits' would result in violence.

I didn't actually borrow any money in 2005, apart from that £30,000 from my dad, which I gave back virtually straight away. Ironically, I had to use that money to pay a really heavy character, whom I knew was the one who'd hurt my dad before and was on the verge of going after him again. My dad would have been furious if he had known that his £30,000 was going to pay off the very guy who'd had a go at him. I still couldn't go to the police because I didn't want to be seen as a grass, although all I was really doing was trying to protect my family.

Luckily, I managed to borrow £30,000 off my mate Elliot to pay my dad back but I never told anyone why I needed the loan in the first place. If I'd talked to them all properly and explained the situation, it would have made life much easier. But I lied out of fear that something might happen to them. I was stuck in the middle of a web of lies because I was trying to prevent any of my friends and family being hurt.

In early 2006, I met a shadowy figure called Charlie, who had come to me via a friend of mine. Charlie had given my friend a Cartier watch as a Christmas present, even though they hadn't done any work together. That gives you an idea of the sort of manipulative person Charlie was. He thought everyone had a price.

Charlie was a very cool character, who came across as an immensely rich man. To the outside world, he could not have looked less like a criminal, yet that was exactly what he was.

I've used the word 'hindsight' a lot in my life but I keep looking back on this sort of stuff and thinking, 'Why did I allow myself to be pulled into it all?' I should have sold Charlie a flashy watch, shaken his hand and been on my way. But the trouble was I could smell the money on him and the chance of doing business with him. I knew he was a chancer prepared to take on high-risk deals for high returns.

The second time I met Charlie, I delivered a Cartier to him and then happened to mention that I had a contact with around £50,000 worth of watches that could be bought for £25,000. Naturally, his antenna went up instantly.

Charlie liked to control everyone around him. And, of course, I knew from my mate that Charlie had some funds available and anyone like that was of potential use to me. So that's how I found myself sitting in Charlie's swish office in the heart of posh Mayfair.

Charlie wouldn't have known a straight business if it had hit him in the eye, and he told me he was looking to 'invest' in platinum. I quickly realised he and his cronies were basically buying platinum in order to wash money. And it just so happened there was a guy who had £100,000 of my old stock of platinum. I told Charlie I might know someone to buy some of my old stock from and he gave me £100,000 to set up the deal.

So that's how I came to start a limited company in 2005 called 'D Flawless'. I made my cousin Julian the director as I had been struck off. It was a trading company for me to be able to trade watches and metals through. I felt as if I was beginning to get myself re-established workwise.

I told Charlie I could get some platinum in Germany and we agreed a deal to channel it all through me. There was a company in Essex and the idea was to start trading in big numbers of up to £5 million. Potentially, it could turn out to be a massive earner for me.

We were supposed to start with that first proper deal for £100,000 and then the next one would be half-a-million, and it would keep climbing and climbing over the following couple of months. I was supposed to be on 1 per cent, so I could eventually earn £90,000. I didn't want to be clutching at straws so I tried not to get too excited but I knew it was literally a life saver if it all worked out.

Back in the real world, my creditors were still queuing round the block. I handed a lot of that £100,000 I got on that early deal to Den White. He was in the process of buying a house in Spain for cash from a bloke who lived in Essex and I'd pop round to give this guy money.

But at least my main source of income looked as if it was now Charlie. Den White believed that his money had helped start me off with Charlie, so he was happy protecting me on the basis that I would keep him sweet.

Meanwhile, my other 'protector' Ali was continually trying to organise meetings because he knew I'd have to pay him for each one he pulled off. He thought he'd earn enough money to buy a house if it all went well. But he never did and he no doubt blamed me for it. Once again, people I was supposed to trust were simply picking pieces off me and none of them really cared whether I lived or died.

14

LAST-CHANCE SALOON

During the first half of 2006, I made quite a few bob out of that platinum business. The gang led by Charlie ended up hitting more than £10 million turnover during the first six months of that year. Then, one day in the middle of 2006, Charlie called me and said he'd been doing his figures and it seemed that I owed him £700,000. OK – I admit I did skim £150,000 off some of the deals, but not the £700,000 he was claiming.

Naturally, I insisted I didn't owe him anything but I knew I was in deep shit yet again. Charlie said on the phone I had to go in for a meeting with him. I knew I had no choice in the matter.

Charlie had a couple of heavies in his office when I arrived there, plus a very muscly-looking, little Indian bodybuilder fellow who seemed to be his main minder. I told Charlie very calmly that I needed to do all my figures to try to work out why there was this 'discrepancy'.

Phew. He agreed to give me a chance to sort things out. That's when he dropped an even bigger bombshell. It turned out the money that he claimed was missing belonged to one of Britain's most feared and notorious underworld bosses. I gulped for air when he said that, but tried not to give away the fact I was shitting myself. I now realised for the first time that all that money he'd been washing through the platinum deals belonged to probably the single most powerful crime family in Britain.

I left that meeting in a complete panic. I knew I was in deep trouble because characters like this villain really did shoot first and ask questions later. Mind you, Charlie might have been saying all that just to scare me into paying the money, but I somehow doubted it. His claims had the ring of truth about them because I knew Charlie had those sorts of criminal connections.

So I phoned Den White and asked him to come over from his home in Marbella for a meeting with Charlie and his people. Luckily, Den still saw me as a worthwhile 'investment', so he was prepared to keep batting on my behalf. I explained the situation to Den and, instead of being scared by the mere mention of the name of the underworld family, he seemed to relish the idea of some contact with them.

'I'll sort it out, Jason,' he said, as calm as the proverbial cucumber.

It later turned out that Den had already fallen out big-time with a particularly nasty member of the family but I didn't know all that at the time.

'Fuck 'em,' added Den.

So, a few days later, we trotted over to see Charlie again, knowing full well that one of the world's most deadly gangsters was going to put a bullet in me if I didn't sort this mess out very quickly.

Den packed some CS gas and I have to say he is quite an impressive-looking fellow. He's 6ft, very muscular and an ex-boxer. Anyway, we got to Charlie's office and initially Charlie was very calm and polite. But it was obvious to me from the get-go that Den had some 'pull' when it came to facing down these sorts of problems and he wasn't afraid to show his cards very quickly, either.

Den ignored Charlie's greasiness and immediately got down to business by saying to Charlie, 'We will sort this out but you cannot dictate terms to us.'

I was astonished because Charlie kept his calm, despite the way Den was speaking to him in such an intimidatory manner. Within a few minutes, Charlie agreed to let me go away and try to work out the figures once again. More breathing space.

I realised there and then the value of having Den present, although, as we left, one of Charlie's 6ft-plus bodyguards did whisper in my ear, 'If you pull any more scams, you'll be in real shit.'

I nodded and smiled, but inside I was bricking it because I knew this lot wouldn't let me get away with anything.

As we left the building, Den turned to me and said, 'Fuck me, Jason. Any more skeletons in the closet?'

As it happened, there were plenty more where that one came

from, including creditor Mark, whom we were going to meet that very afternoon.

I was due to see Mark at the Prince Regent Hotel in Chigwell. Den and I turned up just as Mark walked into the reception with three of the scariest-looking blokes I have ever seen in my life. One of them was a chilling-looking character covered in tattoos called Henry Carter, but I didn't find out his name until a lot later.

We all sat down at a small table and Carter seemed particularly menacing. The other two called themselves 'Terry' and 'Wayne'. It turned out that Mark had borrowed money from Terry who happened to be Carter's best friend. Carter knew Den White and said hello to him straight away, which was obviously a relief to me.

Carter said he had meant to call Den White to say they were going to the meeting. But, despite the fact they all seemed to know each other, I did think to myself, 'Fuck me!' It was heavy stuff.

Carter kicked things off by saying, 'Now, about this money you owe.'

I was about to speak when Den interrupted me because he believed Carter was talking to him and he wanted to deal with this. I wasn't going to argue with that.

Den then explained he was talking 'for me'. Den told Carter what was happening and even had the gall to say to him, 'I ain't scared of you.'

But I fucking was. I was completely and utterly convinced they were going to take me away with them that afternoon and there was nothing Den could do to stop them. I really couldn't see any way out of this one.

They turned round and looked at Den as if he was completely, fucking crazy after his outburst, but for some reason they didn't all reach for their sawn-offs.

Instead, Carter chipped in very calmly, 'He owes £220,000.'

Then Den snapped back: 'It's up to Mark who he owes the money to.'

Carter said, 'No it ain't. He *has to* pay that money.'

I didn't like the emphasis on the words '*has to*'.

Somehow, we agreed some sort of 'payment plan' that afternoon. Den even volunteered that he would get me to pay the money off out of what I owed him; we settled on a figure of £6,000 a month. In hindsight (how often do I wish it was available at the time?), I should have stood up and said I didn't owe them any money whatsoever because I'd borrowed the money from Mark, not Carter's friend Terry.

This was a typical example of why I should never have borrowed money from 'the street' in the first place. Debts were just passed around from hand to hand. I felt railroaded because I knew in the back of my mind that the Indian platinum scheme was the only way I could earn any money but now Charlie was after £700,000 from me, which he claimed was owed to a major villain. What a mess.

We ended the meeting that afternoon by shaking hands. I would pay Den and then Den would hand it to them. But I was in even more shit, as usual. Mind you, without Den's involvement, they'd probably have just dragged me away and shot me, although it's true to say that I would never have gone to the meeting in the first place without Den.

I came out of there feeling very wobbly. I'd gone through two incredibly heavy meetings on the same day. The pressure was almost unbearable. I felt as if I'd been cornered and there was no means of escape. Not even a chink of light at the end of the tunnel.

It was made even worse when the platinum Indians decided to pay my poor sister a call just to remind me to hurry up and sort out the missing £700,000 they claimed I owed them. This time, instead of opening her front door when they came knocking, she sensibly leaned out of the bedroom window. There were three or four blokes outside and they told her in no uncertain terms to tell me not to fuck them about. Yet again, I felt very bad about my family being dragged into my shit.

It took me a day or two to work out it was the Indians who'd harassed my sister and then I called Charlie. He was most apologetic and claimed it was all a mistake. I doubted it very much. He wanted me to realise they were deadly serious about the money I owed them – or rather to a renowned villain – as they claimed.

Charlie put on his usual greasy front and even said to me, 'I apologise. They shouldn't have done that.'

But I knew precisely the game they were playing. They gave these little 'warnings' to me to let me know they were 'thinking about me'. Another time, Charlie rang me to tell me he had my mum's phone number. They liked giving the impression they could find out anything they wanted about me. Maybe they could or maybe they couldn't – one thing was for sure, I wasn't going to put them to the test to find out.

That's when I decided that I needed to sit down with somebody who was on the same level as these heavy characters. Then it came to me – the best person to do that was Henry Carter. He'd even told me at that very first meeting that I was being bullied into paying money that I didn't owe in the first place. I liked his approach, even though I was supposed to be a victim when we first encountered each other.

Henry was an intriguing character. Despite looking really frightening, he rarely had to resort to physical force. Just seeing him scared most people witless. He just walked in a room and you knew he meant business. It's a very effective look and it's served him very well down the years.

Henry was a person that criminal families went to in order to recover debts. He was the top man in his field. His name really did mean something in the underworld. He also had a team of people who were really aggressive and horrible and, as they say in the trade, 'He gets the job done.'

So I decided that one day I would get Henry on my side. I owed Henry's client a lot of money and I was getting constant phone calls from him, including some very chilling threats. His classic line on the phone was: 'You must start paying this money, Jay, or else it is all going to start going the wrong way for you.'

But in the back of my mind I'd already decided that I would

choose my moment and try to persuade him to help me, but first I had to prove I could pay off his client.

During the summer of 2006, Den White tried to encourage me to move to Marbella with my family. I didn't fancy it, although we went there on holiday and loved it. But I didn't want to bring up my kids there. It was tempting to run away, though.

When I got back from holiday, I got a message from Den White saying we'd been summoned to a meeting with a guy called Craig from Dartford who was the right-hand man of a notorious London crime family and he was apparently the main 'investor' when it came to the £700,000 Charlie and the Indians claimed I owed them. The meeting was to discuss the 'figures' I'd earlier said I was going to calculate in response to their accusations that I had nicked their money.

The meeting was to be held at a house in Loughton owned by a mate of this guy. Then, out of the blue, Den said he couldn't come with me but he assured me they would not try anything heavy and I reluctantly agreed to go on my own, although obviously I wasn't keen.

So I turned up at this big mansion, which belonged to a criminal called Rog who'd just got out of prison. Strangely, there were no cars outside the house but all the main characters, including Charlie, were there waiting for me inside, plus this Craig bloke. Luckily, he turned out to be the same guy I'd sold that watch to at the service station near Dartford Tunnel a year earlier. He didn't recognise me at first, but now I wanted him to know I hadn't gone running to the police. He immediately said he was grateful to me for not landing them in it when the police turned up at that earlier meet.

But then this guy Craig got straight down to business. 'So, Jason … what's going on with this money?'

Despite his earlier friendliness, I had a definite feeling something was about to happen to me. It was an intimidating atmosphere. At least six of them were standing around a huge dining-room table and I'd walked in on my own. Lee was a friend of Den's, but I didn't know him well and he'd remained outside the meeting, which was also a bit ominous.

Simon then said to me, 'Don't worry, mate. We promised Lee you could leave this meeting.'

Presumably that meant they weren't going to kidnap or kill me, I thought to myself.

Then Craig added, 'But we are going to let you explain yourself. We don't want any more lies.' That's when they told me I owed them £750,000 and I had to pay it. They didn't even bother to explain why it had leapt up another fifty grand since my last meeting with Charlie.

As I mentioned earlier, I knew I owed them money but I thought it was about £150,000 maximum and I had all the figures to talk them through my calculations, but I was all on my own and it didn't seem like the right moment to challenge them. And, at the back of my mind, I knew I didn't even have £150,000 to give them, let alone the £750,000 they claimed I owed them.

Charlie then steamed right into Den White's reputation in his absence. That set yet more alarm bells ringing. I was in a very vulnerable situation. I also started to wonder why Den wasn't at the meeting. Something was wrong. I should never have been left to go to this meeting alone.

My priority was to get out of that house in one piece. So I told them I would be sending them £70,000 over the next couple of days and I would work out the figures for the rest of the money very carefully.

Then Charlie snapped at me, 'You have three days to come up with all the figures, OK? We meet again in three days.'

I was so relieved to get out of that house in one piece that I didn't even think about the implications of finding that money and showing them some dodgy paperwork to try to convince them I didn't owe £750,000.

Later that same day, I got together with my dad because it was a Jewish holiday. I was in the biggest trouble I had ever been in and I needed some fatherly advice and understanding. We sat down and tried to work out all the true figures that I owed the Indians. It really was a last throw of the dice.

Ever since all that awful business when Dad was attacked, he'd helped me without any hesitation. He'd been outraged at the intimidation that was going on and he was determined not to let the bullies rule my life. That makes him a pretty special dad by anyone's standards.

We eventually worked out there was a disparity of at least £200,000 in the figures provided by Charlie and the Indians. But I still wasn't sure I'd got the figures totally right yet. So I called Charlie and tried to get an extension on the date of the next meeting, but he refused. Then Den announced he wouldn't be coming back from Spain for that meeting, either, which meant I was even more vulnerable to attack.

But Den said that yet again they'd given their word they would do nothing to me, although I knew only too well that, if I turned up without a proper offer, I would be fucked.

I kept hearing Charlie's voice from the last meeting when he snapped at me, 'If you make up any paperwork, you ain't fuckin' walking out of here alive.'

With those threatening voices going round and round in my head, I set off for the next meeting with Charlie and the Indians feeling very shaky about everything. It seemed like I was driving into a minefield. At the very least, I was going to get a beating, or maybe something even worse … like a bullet in the head.

15

A GLIMMER
OF HOPE

I got close to the rendezvous point – a service station on th M25 – but couldn't bring myself to exit the motorway because I was so scared of what I was driving into. So I began driving my rental car up and down the M25 rather than go to the meeting. I just couldn't bring myself to turn off the motorway. I knew I had to think of some way of getting out of that meeting. So, for the moment, I just kept going back and forth between junctions 28 and 29 over and over again.

The tension was building up so much that I was shaking like a leaf and I had a band of pain running right through my head like someone had plunged a knife in one ear and it was coming out the other side. It got so bad I felt almost like stopping the car on the hard shoulder and just running away. I couldn't escape the fact that I was heading into a dead end in every sense of the word.

I even began to imagine my own funeral happening in front of my very eyes.

I had to find a way to get out of the meeting.

Then, out of my madness and fear, came a brilliant, but demented idea. I'd drive into the back of a lorry in a deliberate accident. I was serious. It would be risky but nowhere near as risky as going to that meeting.

Looking back on it (with more bloody hindsight!), I must have been completely potty at the time because it was such a risky strategy. But all I could think of back then as the minutes were ticking away was what they would do to me.

So, as I hurtled down the M25, I began looking out for a suitable lorry to crash into. And all the time I was thinking, 'This is going to help me avoid being either killed, kidnapped or at the very least terrorised.' I was shaking so much by now I had to grip tightly on to the steering wheel, my eyes snapping around looking for the right vehicle to hit.

And all the time I was visualising the 'accident' in my head because I knew there would be a thin line between achieving my aim, but avoiding serious injury or even death at the same time.

Then I thought maybe I should leave the motorway at the next roundabout and sit on the roundabout and wait for a lorry to smash into. I indicated left and went up the ramp and then parked the car with its hazard lights flashing and waited ... and waited ... and waited. But every time a lorry drove by, something made me hesitate. I didn't have the balls to do it. I must have watched at least a dozen trucks sail past. I was also worried about causing any injury or damage to other people.

So I drove back on to the motorway, settled in the centre lane and decided to try a different tactic. Maybe, I thought to myself, it would work better if I drove into the back of a lorry in the slow lane.

Just then, I spotted a big articulated truck alongside me. I moved across to the slow lane and drove right up behind it. I stayed just a couple of feet close to it for what seemed like ages wondering when I should pick my moment.

Then his brake lights went on as he suddenly slowed down for something ahead. This was surely the perfect moment? I slammed my foot down on the accelerator and sat back as my rental car surged towards the rear of the lorry.

Everything then seemed to go into slow motion.

I've never been so thankful for my seatbelt as the front of the rental car clipped the corner of the back of the lorry. I skidded out of control, braking *after* I'd hit it. I struggled to steer the car as it veered left into the hard shoulder. Then it hit the embankment and slammed to a halt.

I sat in the car in a complete daze, then I looked up and noticed that the lorry I'd hit had braked hard and was now pulling over on to the hard shoulder after another motorist had flagged it down. The driver jumped out of his cab immediately and seemed very concerned. Poor bloke … it wasn't his fault. I tried to move and realised that, thankfully, there were no serious injuries. But I was so shaken up about the meeting that I guess I was in a form of shock.

The lorry driver turned out to be foreign and he leaned into my window to ask me if I was OK. I nodded slowly as if I was in pain. Obviously, he had no idea I'd just deliberately crashed into him. He wasn't even angry with me for going into the back of his lorry.

The driver then called for an ambulance on his mobile as he remained standing next to my car. I presumed they'd most probably take me to a north London rather than an east London hospital as the crash had occurred between Enfield and Potters Bar. That would suit me perfectly.

I made out I was slightly concussed. The ambulance turned up very quickly and I was helped out of the car by a paramedic. Then, just as I got in the ambulance, the strangest thing happened. All my phones starting ringing.

I pretended not to be interested and ignored all my phones. Then it dawned on me that this was a perfect opportunity to put myself in the clear, as far as that heavyweight meeting was concerned. I encouraged the ambulanceman to answer one of the mobiles. It turned out to be one of the gangsters I was about to meet at that service station.

'He's been involved in an accident and we are in the ambulance on the way to hospital,' the paramedic told the caller.

I found out later that Den then got a call from the same gangster to say I'd had an accident. Den then called my father, which was not so good because the last thing I wanted to do was put him through it when it was all a mad scam to avoid being seriously injured or perhaps even killed by a bunch of criminals.

I hated putting my dad through that sort of angst for no reason, but there was no way at that time to tell him the truth.

I ended up staying in hospital all that afternoon and Den White even flew over from his home in Marbella to see me. That 'bought' me three extra days to sort things out.

But, looking back on it, that accident was even – by my standards – one of the most shameful things I have ever done. I was obviously having some kind of breakdown but that was no excuse for putting my family through all that worry and fear. Not to mention wasting all the valuable time of the emergency services. Yet there is another side of me that believes that, if I had not pulled that stunt, I really would have been killed.

The police only turned up at the scene of the accident after I had already been 'rushed' to hospital, which was rather handy. I have never admitted to anyone before that it was a faked accident. I'm not proud of it but, the way I look at it, I didn't have much choice in the matter.

There was virtually no damage to the lorry, although the rental car was badly smashed up with a crushed front wing from where I'd gone into the back of that truck. Of course, I didn't give a fuck about the accident. It had simply given me three days' breathing space that I desperately needed. In that time, I worked out I owed the Indians just £90,000 and produced all the paperwork to prove it. The figures they were talking about were rubbish and I now had the evidence to prove I was right.

But I also knew only too well that the next meeting would be a virtual kangaroo court, although at least I had something to show them. Den White came to that meeting this time. Charlie insisted it was held at another of his plush offices, in Mayfair, right next door to the American Embassy in Grosvenor Square.

But, when we arrived, there was no sign of Charlie. Instead, that same little, muscly Indian guy with big arms was there, as well as Craig, that 'associate' of the notorious London crime family. He also had with him his bodyguard, who apparently used to be a kick-boxing champion. There was another muscly guy who looked like somebody out of a Guy Ritchie gangster film. We'd been given assurances that we would be safe at this meeting, but that didn't stop me thinking when I walked in, 'Fuckin' hell, this is not good.'

The fact Charlie was 'running late' and the meeting had started without him was another ominous warning sign to me. Luckily, all the heavies seemed to know Den personally. There were lots of hugs all round. It annoyed Craig that his people were so friendly with Den, but it was great news for me, obviously.

Craig then took a deep, ominous breath and started laying into me. 'I'm telling you now if you pull out one bit of moody paper or lie or anything that comes out of your mouth ain't true, then I swear to you, I don't care what anyone has told you, you ain't leaving this room.'

I knew then and there that, if I showed them all this paperwork and they thought it was a con, they'd kill me. But I remained convinced that my version was genuine.

So now it was my turn to take a deep breath. I pulled out a spreadsheet, which showed all the money that had gone in and out on the platinum deals. I was bricking myself but they all seemed a bit blinded by my figures, which was encouraging.

Anyway, I came up with a £90,000 figure as opposed to the £700,000-plus they'd claimed and they seemed quite chilled about it all, which was even more surprising. The muscly little Indian kept trying to speak but I cut over the top of him and just repeatedly tried to assure them all that the paperwork was 100 per cent genuine.

Just then Charlie finally turned up and I took a big gulp because I fully expected him to rubbish everything I was saying. But the little Indian and the others immediately told him I owed them just £90,000, according to the figures. Charlie looked at them for a few moments. I was still waiting for a verbal backlash at the very least.

But instead Charlie smiled at me. 'Why didn't you produce all this paperwork earlier?'

I smiled back and explained that was why I needed more time.

Then he turned to the little Indian and the other heavies. 'Fuck me, boys … guess we're not going to buy the Roller today after all then!'

The others laughed politely along with Charlie.

'So when are you going to pay the ninety grand?' asked Charlie, in an even more relaxed voice.

I still couldn't quite believe what I was hearing. I was tempted to try to explain to them that their figures were still wrong but then decided not to push my luck. After all, I had just gone from owing nearly £800,000 to £90,000.

Then Charlie repeated his question. 'So, Jason, when can you pay the £90,000?'

They all looked mightily irritated when I hesitated at that moment.

One of the heavies then chipped in, 'And don't start making fuckin' promises you cannot keep either.'

I said obviously I didn't have the £90,000 in one lump sum to pay them. 'But I can give you two grand in a month's time and I'll pay it down from there.'

Incredibly, they agreed to it.

They obviously wouldn't have seen it this way, but they looked like idiots in front of Den because they'd completely backed down. Den had told them I was all right and they were having to admit he was right. We all shook hands on the £90,000 deal but then I kept wondering if Charlie might just bollock his team and start picking the deal to bits.

We had a driver waiting outside for us after we left that office and, as we got in the car, Den said, 'Are you relieved?'

'Not half!'

I'd also looked good in front of Den because I knew he'd been doubting me.

'You done well, son,' he said, clapping me on the back. 'I am proud of you. I'm pleased you didn't bullshit them and stuff. I know you'll pay the money off and that will be the end of that.'

I presume Charlie had to stump up some of that missing money to the big crime family but I suspect he owed them it from other 'business deals' and had been simply trying to bully me into taking on that debt. These were the sort of deadly games I had started taking almost for granted.

But then Charlie was hardly scraping the barrel himself. We're talking about a man with four very flash cars. The guy was an out-and-out multi-millionaire, with fingers in all sorts of pies.

Following the Charlie meeting, I got our driver to drop me off home. I told my wife and my dad about what had happened and they were so relieved. It really did seem like a pivotal point. I'd taken the gangsters on at their own game and won. What a result!

That Friday night, I went to my sister's house for dinner and was feeling more relaxed than I had felt for years. It was so nice to be among my family and their 'normal' lives after a very dodgy few months.

Then, at about 7.00 that evening, the phone went and I saw Charlie's name come up on the screen. I thought to myself, 'Oh no … here we go again.'

I almost ignored it but something made me decide to pick it up. I went out into the garden to take the call and Charlie said he'd been going through all the figures and it wasn't quite as straightforward as it had at first seemed. Then he tried to say the invoices from six months before were all 1 per cent incorrect, which meant if you added it all up it came to £900,000 that was missing. Somehow I stayed calm and pointed out that surely the invoices would have been corrected when they were submitted originally.

Charlie then said he had gone through £9 million worth of invoices from six months earlier. It was all complete and utter bollocks since they had still clearly earned more than £1 million worth of profit. I told Charlie we should talk about it again on the following Monday.

Then I called Den who made a series of calls on my behalf and even told Charlie and his cronies, 'We've agreed ninety grand and there is no going back on it.'

In reality, there was no way that Charlie could pull invoices that had been raised six months earlier and claim each one was wrong. I reckon Charlie was just trying to get some brownie points and maybe recapture a little pride in the process.

They upped the £2,000 a month to £25,000 a month until the whole £90,000 was paid back. Then they tried a classic con and claimed I was £5,000 short on the first payment.

That made me think about Henry Carter. He seemed to be the sort of character who might be the key to sorting out my mess. I knew that, once I started paying the debt off, they'd try every trick in the book, including this very tactic saying I was giving them short amounts of cash. Den was in Spain most of the time so I called Henry and asked him if he knew these guys. He said he knew them well, so I decided he was the man who could help keep me alive.

Henry helped me broker the repayment deal. Charlie was once again trying to take the piss out of me. After about six months, I paid all the £90,000 back and that was the end of the matter, thank goodness.

But it always seemed as if there was another drama lurking somewhere nearby. A few weeks later, I dropped off £20,000 at some bloke's house. A couple of minutes later, I got a call saying I'd only left him £15,000. Here we go, I thought, this is what they're going to be like with me from now on. It was as if Charlie and his boys had put the word around that I was not to be trusted. Thank goodness I'd brought Henry on board.

I'd never forgotten how scary Henry had seemed at our first meeting. The fact that Henry had a very flat, unemotional voice was very effective. He wasn't even very good with words, but the tattoos were there for everyone to see and they certainly seemed to do the trick!

Den had even told me that Henry was a genuine face, which meant he got the utmost respect wherever he went. After that first meeting, I had immediately started paying the money and Henry was the one who'd call me to make sure the cash was on its way. That's how I started to get to know him. Henry loved the phone and we really hit it off, despite the fact he was supposed to be threatening me with death if I didn't continue paying off that debt.

Henry was a great believer in the power of the phone. He'd always be buying pay-as-you-go phones for £20 each on the basis that most of the time you can call a punter without bothering with a meeting and then just chuck the phone away to make sure no one can retrace your footsteps. As he once said, 'Jason, it can all be said on a phone and then you just throw it away. Simple as that.'

He was dead right, of course.

As I began building some kind of rapport with Henry, I

started to tell him all about my arrangement with Den. Henry reckoned Den was taking the piss out of me. We totted up that he had had £700,000 off me through various deals down the years, so no wonder he tried to make me feel as if I couldn't survive without him.

Henry told me he would do it a different way and only take a very small percentage of the money I owed and he'd guarantee all my pay-offs went smoothly. I was still in one hell of a hole, so a bloke like Henry could well be the answer to all my problems in the long term. I had to sort these people out before it really did cost me my life.

16
FAMILY SNAPS

My new 'protector' Henry had a shaven head and looked like a typical 1980s skinhead. He always called me Jason and when he did talk (which was rare) he tended to sound a bit like a punch-drunk school kid. He even seemed a little 'slow', but that was all an act, as I was soon to discover.

Henry recognised I was a reasonably smart bloke but he also knew perfectly well I was not a criminal. He said he wished he'd met me five years earlier because then we'd both have got very wealthy because he would never have allowed some of these characters to lure me into so much debt. His attitude was always: 'Get this paid off, Jason, and I'll make sure he doesn't come after you for anything else.'

Obviously, it was very reassuring to have someone like Henry on my side.

At the start of 2007, I met up with a chap called Jerry. His dad

Fred had been a gangster in the 1960s. The old man had recently died of asbestos poisoning, otherwise I might well have gone to him about all my 'problems' because he'd been a serious underworld kingpin.

Jerry looked on me as a kind of father figure, and he told me he had a rich mate based in Thailand called Ben who wanted to do some big-money deals. Naturally, I was all ears.

So, in January 2007, I went to Jerry's house in London to meet an associate of Ben's who described himself as his 'financier'. This guy was about 5ft 8in but looked muscly and strong like a light-middleweight boxer. He was well dressed in a suit with spiky hair and stank of aftershave. He also happened to have a brand-new five series diesel BMW. I was always looking for people with money so I could invest it in platinum deals and obviously borrow it for my own purposes. I knew how to buy and sell platinum very lucratively, but I didn't have the funds. So, when anyone rich came along, it was perfect.

Anyway, Ben's associate said Ben would put £200,000 into me and he expected me to give him 10 per cent a month return on a platinum deal. So I took this fella's £200,000 and decided it was time to drop Den completely by paying him off with £150,000 of that money. Ben's mate in turn raised more money on top of the £200,000 to lend to me and this time he never even told Ben about it.

I knew perfectly well that Den had got a house and a £70,000 Porsche to pay for, and once he had paid off those two 'necessities' then he'd be out of my life.

I'd gained a lot more confidence having Henry behind me. He was a much better option than Den because he was a constant presence and, as the word got round that he was on my side, people started treating me with more respect.

So I paid off the house and Porsche for Den and told him I was going to take a step back. The guy had earned something like £750,000 off me and half-a-million of that was probably clear profit. But, like a lot of these people, he was only telling me what he wanted me to hear.

Then, around this time, I met a guy who knew some of the other faces who'd already lent me loads of cash. He told me he had some gold from Peru and talked about a great deal to sell it. I was soon hooked in.

This guy invested £250,000 into a gold deal; this should have saved my bacon, although I soon realised he had given his money up front to purchase gold from Africa. It was then that I knew he'd been screwed – you can't part with money up front for gold, as they will take your investment and you'll never see it again.

It was September 2007 and we were once more enjoying our Jewish holiday all at home as a family. But I had been borrowing more money right, left and centre, and, as so often happened, my other life soon caught up with me and turned a joyous occasion into a nightmare. I got a text from a criminal called Ted saying, if I didn't pay him the money I owed him, he'd be at my house at 7.30 that evening. I hadn't given him anything for a few months so it was hardly surprising he was after me. But I was desperate to avoid a scene in front of my wife and kids, so I got very stressed waiting for him to turn up by standing near the window and getting jumpy every time a car drove slowly past the house.

But, in the end, Ted didn't turn up that night, so I went to bed relieved but fully aware that he would be on to me again soon. Then, next morning at 7.30am, the doorbell went. Thank God Nic didn't hear it; I slipped downstairs to answer it and there was Ted. He looked like a boxer dog with a bald head and a flat nose. Another bloody gangster out of central casting.

'Hello, Jason.'

I invited Ted in and made him a cup of coffee. It was a mad thing to do with my family all upstairs, but it seemed the best way to try to defuse the potentially dangerous situation.

Then I took an even bigger gamble and told him, 'Ted, you're always welcome in my house for a cuppa, but the bottom line is that I don't have any money at the minute.'

Ted stayed calm, thank God. 'I can't wait for ever, Jason.'

'I know that, Ted, but I simply don't have it at the moment. I can't be more honest than that.'

Ted seemed to appreciate my honesty and I promised him I would be in touch within the next couple of weeks with some money. I don't know why I said that, because I hadn't a clue where any money would come from.

So Ted accepted my story and left the house, driving off in his brand-new 4x4.

I tell this story because you need to understand how much all this pressure was building on me. There was no escape from it. I was ducking and diving from one debt to the next without any respite. And the cold, hard reality was that there was no real light at the end of the tunnel. The only thing I could see happening was my own impending death at the hands of one of these gangsters.

In the middle of all this, my domestic life started to come crashing down around my ears. My sister-in-law Simone and her husband Barry's youngest child had tragically developed a brain tumour. We'd had a poor relationship with them for a long time, but I decided now was the perfect moment to break the ice because they needed support at such a difficult time.

So I sent my sister-in-law a text saying: 'No matter what's gone on in the past, I only wish that your daughter is OK.'

They were obviously grateful because I got a text back from my brother-in-law asking us round to their house on a Sunday afternoon. I hoped it would mark a reconciliation with Nic's family. I hadn't seen much of them for a long time and I wanted us all to be friends again.

I hadn't paid the rent on our house for months and we were going to be chucked out on to the street soon if I didn't come up with somewhere new to live. So I decided to ask my brother-in-law if he would lend me some money to rent a new house.

I'd helped him out with a spot of personal bother so this time he couldn't refuse, but he insisted on certain conditions in relation to me paying him the money back. The other reason I persuaded him to lend me some money was because he'd made £70,000 out of one of my other deals. So, armed with a loan from Barry, I was able to pay all six months' rent in advance on a new home. Once again, we had just managed to avoid the scrapheap … but for how much longer?

Around this time, I got involved in helping people exchange currency for euros through a couple of dodgy characters I'd borrowed money from in the past. I would earn a couple of per cent for doing it. That meant on fifty grand I could earn a grand. Not huge money by any means, but any cash that I could earn and wasn't borrowed was vital. I was literally taking a bag of cash and then handing them back another bag of cash in a different currency.

The trouble is it was tempting to dip into those bags of cash because I needed to pay back money to the sinister Ben based in Thailand to whom I owed a fortune from those so-called 'platinum deals'.

Once, I really took the mickey (even by my standards) and swiped £25,000 out of a bag containing £50,000. Once again, I used it to pay off Ben but all it did was buy me a little time but it hardly made a dent in what I owed him. It was reckless stupidity on my part. I shouldn't have taken the money because it belonged to the guy who was supposed to pay me 1 per cent commission and he was more than capable of coming after me.

But there always seemed to be even bigger, more dangerous problems on the horizon. I think that's why I often took such huge risks. Eventually, I decided to tell Ben I couldn't pay him off any more and he went ballistic. He said there was no way I could walk away from the debt and I had no choice but to pay it because it was simply not going to go away.

I also owed a friend a bucketload of cash. Jamie acted like he was my best friend but he'd insisted on turning a £30,000 loan into a £90,000 debt virtually overnight. That's not exactly 'friendly', is it?

Not surprisingly, I gave this friend the runaround for ages. I felt he'd taken advantage of me in many ways, even though I should have known better and I was well aware of the 'rules' of the game.

In the meantime, I had a 'normal' family life to deal with as well. Nic had decided to hold a Hallowe'en party at our house for a load of the children's school friends. I'd just had a horrible day where it felt as if the whole world was after me for millions of pounds. Anyway, I walked into the Hallowe'en party and there were all these screaming kids and I had to pretend to enjoy it, which wasn't easy. By the time most of the kids had left, it was 9.00pm and I was feeling worn out and desperate for something to eat.

I was just about to sit down in the kitchen when my wife announced that this mate had turned up at the front door; he had no clue how fucked up I was mentally. The years were now well and truly catching up with me and, to be honest, I just wanted to go to sleep and not wake up. I lost my appetite all of a sudden. We greeted each other with a nod of the head and a 'hello, mate' and then he sat down in the kitchen with Nic and let rip at me. He said I was a 'lying piece of shit' and that I'd had more money off him and I never stopped lying.

It was embarrassing in front of my own wife to hear these sorts of accusations. But I tried to stay calm and told him, 'I'll get the money for you tomorrow. You can pick it up from here.'

Of course, I didn't have a penny to give him but I somehow had to buy myself time.

But it wasn't the money that was the *real* problem. Seconds after he had left the house, Nic turned on me. 'I want you out … I want you out of the house.'

I was stunned. This was the first time she'd uttered those words, despite all those earlier incidents, when my money problems had threatened the one thing I valued more than anything else – my wife and family. I tried to convince Nic that my so-called mate was just taking the piss and that he'd already had some money off me. She didn't look as if she believed me, so I changed tactics and said, 'I'm not going anywhere.'

For some weird reason, that got Nic to calm down a bit. Well, at least she didn't carry on trying to get me to leave the house. We eventually went to bed that night, although the atmosphere was still awful. I knew I'd crossed yet another line. How much more could I get away with?

I lay awake all night dreading the next day, because my 'mate' was due round and I had that nasty piece of work Ben after me as well. I felt awful. I didn't know which way to turn.

As I lay there in bed, waiting for the sun to come up, I feared that this time I probably had really blown it all … and I wondered whether there really were any escape routes left.

17
CRY FOR HELP

I finally managed to nod off in the early hours but then woke up in a cold sweat at dawn. We had a loft room in the house so I decided to go up there to make some calls so no one could hear me. I was shaking and sweating and had this feeling of doom that just wouldn't go away.

It was 1 November 2007, and at 7.00am I called my GP, Dr White, and told him, 'I am standing here and I am about to take a load of tablets. I don't really want to but this is a cry for help and I need to go somewhere for a few days.'

I didn't actually have any tablets in my hand and, of course, one part of me just wanted to get off the street to avoid my pursuers. I just prayed that my family would support me if I had to be admitted somewhere.

Dr White replied, 'Suppose the ambulance doesn't turn up in time?'

It was a good point since he thought I was about to knock back a load of tablets.

I said, 'OK, OK … I hear what you're saying.'

He then asked me to ring him back in ten minutes while he made 'some calls'.

He was soon back on the line again, having booked me into a rehab clinic in Lisson Grove. 'Are you capable of getting yourself there?'

I assured him I was.

I put the phone down and I went downstairs to our bedroom and woke up Nic.

'Listen, I've got something to tell you. I just called Dr White and I am going into rehab. I can't do all this lying any more. I just cannot cope with it. I am worried I am going to ruin our marriage and destroy everybody around me.'

Bleary-eyed, Nic looked up at me and actually smiled. That's when I knew I was making the right decision. She didn't want a husband who lied to her all the time, even though in my mind I had been protecting her from the truth because it was so dangerous.

So I got in the car and drove myself across London to rehab. I was relieved because I thought I'd be safe from all those criminals who were after me. It was my way of escaping the pressures. It was certainly better than any other alternative I could think of.

I tried to convince myself on the drive over to the clinic that I was right to go and that it was the best thing to do. But then it dawned on me that I also had to be open to it, otherwise it wouldn't be any use to me in real terms.

I parked my black V5 Golf in an NCP car park near the clinic and then strolled in through the entrance. It didn't really feel any different from a hotel or a private hospital. I gave my name at reception and a nurse eventually took me up in the lift and showed me to my bedroom. The moment she closed the door behind her as she left, I felt a deep rush of complete and utter loneliness. I was all on my own.

Within minutes, all my phones went off. It just about summed up the pressures that had been mounting on me. I wanted everyone to know where I was so they'd leave me alone but I couldn't face talking to anyone at that moment. Luckily, my 'mate' had rung Nic that morning and she'd told him that I had gone into rehab. Apparently, he just put the phone down after saying he'd had enough of it. What could he do now?

I did eventually return a call to one gangster I owed money to and told him I was in rehab. I even told him to come and see me in there if he wanted, because I needed everyone to know this was genuine, otherwise they might still go after my family.

The response was pretty blunt and to the point: 'You cannot fuckin' run away from this, Jason.'

I replied, 'I'm not running away from it. I just cannot deal with it at the moment and this is my only chance.'

There were other characters circling, including an estate agent mate of mine who'd lent me five grand. I can't remember what it was for and he was worth millions of pounds. He was desperate to get his money back and he was no threat but I had to show him I would pay him back for reasons of pride. I contacted Den White for the first time in ages and asked if he could pay the five grand for me and he said he would. So I phoned the estate agent in Spain and said he could pick it up. At least I hadn't let a mate down.

Den White had sounded genuinely concerned I was in rehab but he also made a chilling point of saying he wanted that five grand back very quickly. I didn't have £500 let alone £5,000 on me so I told Nic to let him have my car in the nearby par park. I was amazed when he agreed and Nic had to come up and get the keys from me, pay the car park fees and take it back for Den to collect. I never heard from Den White again.

Anyway, later on that first night in rehab, Ben – that guy I owed a lot of money to – left a message on my voicemail saying, 'We just watched your wife pulling into the house with the kids.' Then he told me exactly what she was wearing. It sent a chill up my spine but there was nothing I could do except hope that he would not actually go near my family. I had been ignoring his calls all day so it was hardly surprising he'd decided to take action like that.

So I phoned Ben and said, 'I am in rehab. I have had a bit of a breakdown and I had to get away from it all.' I think he believed me because I told him exactly where I was. I said, 'I am just telling you now – I haven't got your money. You can do what you want to me but I haven't got it. I am fucked. There is nothing I can do.'

Ben then warned me that I might be picked up by his crowd of 'west London street people', as he called them. He claimed it was apparently their money I had borrowed. They were not serious criminals but people who put small amounts of cash into things and, if they didn't get their money back, they tended to beat people up.

I listened to all this with a resigned feeling of indifference. I'd been as honest as I could. What else could I do? The phone line went dead after Ben's last sentence.

That same night, my dad phoned my new protector Henry to tell him I was in hospital. Henry then did exactly what I hoped he'd do and started ringing round telling people where I was. But I knew perfectly well that some heavy characters wouldn't give a toss about me being in rehab. But, as I lay there in bed in that clinic, I had this incredible urge to stop lying. I genuinely wanted to sort myself out.

The only people I hoped would come to see me in the clinic were my parents and my wife. But I knew that the clinic's reception had received quite a number of calls asking if I was there. Everyone was checking out the rumours. Who can blame them?

In some ways, going into rehab was one of the most selfish things I have ever done because I was effectively abandoning my wife and leaving her to cope with everything on her own. But, luckily, Nic didn't see it that way. She saw it as a non-selfish act on my part. She was delighted I was going because she believed I was heading for some form of breakdown, although I obviously saw it partly as a way to escape the hoods who were after me.

Obviously, my biggest priority was protecting my wife, family and friends. I'd always lied to survive, in a sense, and I still lie in certain situations to this day. But the only reason I did that was because I needed to protect my family. They don't always appreciate that, but then why should they?

A lot of my friends and family tended to think that, because I still had all my limbs intact and I was walking around in one piece, the threat was not there any more. But that most certainly was *not* the case.

Back in that room in the clinic, I felt that rush of loneliness kick in even harder. On my first full morning, my mobile phones were still going off left, right and centre. But I decided to ignore them from now on, although I did wonder what the hell I was doing in that clinic in the first place.

After getting out of bed, I stood around for ages until this very charming psychiatric nurse came in to see me. I made a joke about being labelled a nutcase. She looked at me strangely but ignored my comment.

I hadn't seen one other patient yet.

Then the nurse produced some kind of case history document from my GP and she began to risk assess me. It seemed strange because I would have thought most suicidal people wouldn't want to admit it anyway. Oh well. I admitted I felt like I wanted to commit suicide but insisted I wasn't actually going to do it. She then asked about my medical history and took my blood pressure.

Of course, one side of me was mightily relieved to be in there because I knew people were after me. One lender had warned me that a much more sinister character – one of the toughest gypsies around – 'wanted a word' because he'd given me some of his money and the gypsy wanted it back. Oh, and I also had twenty grand that belonged to a notorious crooked copper who had a reputation for marking people who crossed him.

To a certain degree, admitting myself into that clinic was a bit like that time I'd crashed the car. I knew I couldn't get out of that situation and I felt completely trapped. So, instead of crashing a car again, I went into rehab. Maybe it really was as simple as that?

Later that first morning, I was seen in my room by the clinic's specialist psychiatrist. He was a male doctor and I didn't like him. I don't think he even vaguely got what I was all about. He was a tall guy with black hair – very Iranian-looking. I felt he didn't really care about me and he seemed a bit of a cold person. He asked about my wife, my kids and my parents. I was 100 per cent truthful to him, even about my money problems.

I was keen to get into a group therapy session because I knew that might help me open up. There were two classes in the morning and afternoon, but the bad news was that I would have to switch off my phone, which maybe wasn't such a bad thing.

So, after the specialist had gone, I walked out of my room and headed towards the therapy group. As I walked in, they all looked up at me. Then one very skinny girl said to me, 'You don't look like you need to be in here.'

I'd walked into the wrong session and I was in an eating disorders group meeting.

When I finally found the right room, there were 12 people

already in there. There was a woman about my mum's age, who was typical, north London Jewish. There was another guy of a similar age and appearance to me and a very big guy, who seemed very aggressive at first and looked a bit like a criminal.

I was simply the new boy on the block, so I sat there and kept very quiet at first, as people started talking about their problems. The lady who was my mum's age was going through a very messy divorce and she couldn't cope and felt suicidal. Meanwhile, the guy my age was a self-harmer and I saw his wrists and hands had been cut to pieces.

I felt a bit of a fake because I wasn't sure if I should even be there because my problems seemed nothing in comparison to these people.

When it came to my turn in that first session, I said, 'My name is Jason ... I am a jeweller and I've got myself into a big financial mess and I've got gangsters after me who want to kill me.'

Everyone looked at me like I was an alien from outer space because I was clearly in a very different situation from all the other people in there. I then explained I was happily married with two great children but I felt like I had been lying for too long to too many close people and I had to change. It was difficult to add much more because I wasn't a drug addict, self-harmer or a sufferer from any of the other 'traditional' conditions. I felt so out of place. Suddenly, the woman next to me who was my mother's age started telling us how she had tried to kill herself by swallowing Duracell batteries.

The one good thing that listening and meeting all these people did for me was open my eyes to other people's genuine problems and give me a much better understanding of those with psychological problems and mental illness.

I can't remember much more of that first day. Most of my group were quite friendly with each other because they were all staying on the floor below me. I was on the floor with most of the anorexic patients and that's why I'd gone into their meeting by mistake in the first place. I'd been shocked because they were nearly all models who'd become anorexic and were aged between 16 and their mid-20s. There was a community lounge where you could watch TV and I got on well with all the eating disorders patients and staff on my floor.

But everything was very regimented. You ate three times a day, always at the same time, and the anorexics were virtually marched in, each with a nurse who had to monitor whether they were eating properly. I felt really sorry for those young girls. They seemed so tragic.

The main problem was that every day in the clinic was like a never-ending 'groundhog' day. Nic came up to see me that first full day I was there, but she was told not to come again for the next three or four days so that I could 'settle in'.

She brought me some clothes as I actually thought I'd only be there for one or two nights at first. I was also quite embarrassed to be in there in a sense. It seemed very unmanly. I felt quite down about it all and my confidence levels dropped the moment I got in there. Nic was used to psychiatrists being around because her mum and sisters had all been through a few tricky periods in their lives, but I'd never in my life been near a therapist or a clinic like this one.

It also soon became clear that some of the other patients simply didn't believe my reasons for being in there. They couldn't comprehend what had been happening to me and how open I was about it. I think they thought I was just making half of it up. That made me feel more vulnerable in many ways. There was this one woman who used to laugh at me when I talked about the criminals I encountered as if I was making it all up. Luckily, I was thick-skinned enough not to take much notice.

But, the following day, the same woman completely changed her attitude towards me and said out of the blue, 'I do believe what's happened to you, Jason.' Then she explained quite openly to the group that a friend of hers who was in the jewellery business had heard all about my problems and had convinced her I was telling the truth. What an outrage! She should have been kicked out immediately for breaking the rules by talking about me to people outside the clinic. It made me feel very insecure and untrusting of the other patients.

I complained about this woman and had a quiet word with a counsellor about her, but I didn't want to cause too much fuss. Strangely enough, I actually quite liked this woman, so I didn't want to get her into any really big trouble.

Then I encountered one psychiatrist in the clinic who actually seemed to understand me. I remember him telling me, 'If you get out of this mess, you will keep going back into it.' He was the only person who 'got' what was happening to me and, of course, he was absolutely right.

The only gangster who visited me in the clinic was the sinister Ben. I'd invited him in there to prove to him I was genuinely sick. It was a bit of a gamble but it had to be done. He wasn't allowed to actually come into the clinic, so I had to arrange to meet next door at a restaurant. I got permission from the clinic staff to go there with him but I was supervised by a male nurse, who just sat at the bar watching us to make sure I didn't run away.

I tried to explain to Ben why I was in this mess. I promised I would sort out everything I owed him once I was out and I'd pay him back. But it didn't seem to reassure him one bit.

Ben then lowered his voice so the male nurse couldn't hear him and said he had people sitting outside in a car who were armed and ready to come in and kill me if he gave them the word. But nothing he could throw at me bothered me. I was in a state of resigned indifference.

I'd only wanted him to come there and see me in this environment in order to try to pacify him. Sure, it was a calculated risk as to how far I could push him. And, of course, once these sorts of characters know there is no hope, then they can get potentially much more dangerous.

But, as our meeting progressed, Ben seemed to calm down after all his earlier threats. He even showed a small touch of concern for me and asked me what had happened. I told him about my recent problems and it was clear he knew I was under a lot of pressure. Many people in the London and Essex underworld had heard that

I did repay money in the end, and I promised Ben I was going to deal with it all. I said I didn't have anything to give him at that moment and I needed a bit of time.

Ben gave me all his bank details. It wasn't exactly an ideal way to aid my recovery – I could have told him to wait until I got out – but I needed to keep these problems away from my family so I wanted to deal with Ben there and then. Ben also promised not to go back to my family house again. He said, 'As long as you don't run off, I'll keep away from them.'

Part of the initial reason for going into rehab had been to escape my pursuers. But what I did genuinely get out of going there was that I began seeing things in a different light and I stopped blaming myself so much.

I'd always thought my dad was wrong not to allow me to file for bankruptcy when I was young but now I realised he was right. In hindsight, he should have been harder on me because it would have taught me a valuable lesson. My mum never saw me in a bad light so unintentionally she made the mess even worse for me, which pains me to say.

But I have to confess that the one thing I didn't stop doing at rehab was lie. Everyone has their own interpretation of what a lie actually is, right? But the truth of it is: a lie is a lie. All this bollocks about white lies and stuff ... big lies ... little lies. It doesn't matter. Once you've lied, you've lied. Every single person in this world has lied at some stage in their life.

We've all grown up surrounded by politicians who lie to us on a daily, if not hourly, basis and these lies go all the way down. You lie about school … you lie about homework. And so it goes on and on.

I had been lying to save my life and even the psychiatrist in rehab asked, 'How can I teach you not to lie when it's about saving your life?' And that was the most honest thing anyone has ever said to me.

Nic came to see me as often as possible, and my parents also came three or four times and were amazingly supportive. Meanwhile, I continued trying to convince my creditors that I really didn't have the money they wanted from me. Why would I go into rehab if I had it?

That creditor 'friend' of mine, who had spoken to me so rudely in front of Nic just before rehab, washed his hands of me, which thankfully meant I never actually heard from him again.

Rehab wasn't a luxury – it was a necessity. For the same reasons as driving into the back of that lorry, I had to do it to buy some time.

18

OLD HABITS DIE HARD

I eventually got out of rehab on a Friday. Part of me didn't want to leave because I actually thought I was starting to deal with my addictive personality. But my insurance wouldn't cover me being there any longer.

The doctor I didn't like much thought I was OK to leave but some of the staff didn't agree. Another two weeks would have done me the power of good, because it might have enabled me to handle everything better when I left. But I had no choice in the end.

My other concern that day was my mum, who was having an operation in another hospital that happened to be just opposite the clinic. So I went straight over to see her. My dad was visiting her so he drove me home after we'd seen Mum.

I felt reasonably upbeat about things after my stay in rehab. But neither my mum nor my dad understood the psychiatric side of things. My dad tried to talk about it on the drive home but I was reluctant because I didn't feel like going into details. I said the old creditors were still after me but I didn't want to worry him too much, so I didn't talk about that much, either.

Nic and the kids were at home when I got back but I was in a strange sort of mood. I suppose in some ways I'd been institutionalised by my stay in the clinic. All of a sudden, I felt vulnerable and exposed once again and I didn't like that feeling. I was also back in 'reality' after a couple of weeks escaping everything and everyone.

I knew I had to make this a new beginning. I needed to start a new chapter in my life. I had to try to be more assertive and sort things out. I still had the notorious Henry Carter as my 'friend' and protector, so surely that would help, wouldn't it?

I'd never imagined that every debt would just disappear while I was in rehab. But, of course, it would have been better if I could have just walked away from all my problems instead of going straight back into the lion's den, so to speak.

The first thing I did on the Monday after getting out of rehab was go and see Henry and he seemed happy to pay money on my behalf and talk to the people who were chasing me. It was very much 'business as usual'.

With regard to Henry, I'd made a decision in rehab never to lie to him because I didn't owe him any money any more so what was the point? It was a good thing as well because I had to learn not to lie automatically for the sake of lying.

Naturally, the sinister Ben was soon on the phone harassing

the life out of me for his money. He was pushing for yet another proper, face-to-face meeting. I knew that nothing but paying him off was going to work, so the last thing I wanted was to meet him.

The trouble with rehab was that it only provided a temporary reprieve from my problems. Once I was back out in the real world again, most of the money vultures were circling ever closer, and there was every chance they would get their prey in the end. I couldn't just get myself locked up in a clinic every time the pressure got too much to bear. I had to do something to sort out this mess but, for the moment, it was back to business as usual, even though I wished they would all go away and leave me alone.

First off, after getting out of rehab I borrowed £50,000 from two 'chaps'. I was supposed to turn that round and pay it back to them within two days. But, of course, I needed it to pay Ben. That was always my problem – the vicious circle was omnipresent and Ben was proving the most deadly figure of all.

I did manage to pay off some of my other heavier pursuers but, of course, I only did that by borrowing off other people. Nothing had changed in that respect.

I was using Henry to speak to some very notorious families but I needed a regular bodyguard and that was where Chi fitted in perfectly. He had a black Range Rover sport and always wore a suit. He was also one of the widest men I have ever seen in my life. His shoulders seemed to brush the frame of every door he walked through.

Our first meeting was in Swiss Cottage. I told him I had been in the wrong with a lot of these creditors and that, before I got involved with him, I wanted him to understand that. I think it shocked him a bit that I was so honest. Anyway, Chi said it would cost me two grand a week to have him as my 'adviser' – one grand for the car and one grand for him.

'That's my charges,' he said, as if we were discussing a plumbing job.

I agreed. After all, this enormous man was going to protect me. I knew I needed it because there were a lot of nasty people looking for me. I even admitted I wasn't sure I could pay him every single week but that didn't seem to bother him.

'Right. Let's get going,' he said.

The first thing we had to do was have a meeting with Ben who'd come to see me when I was in rehab and was an ever-present thorn in my side.

We agreed to meet Ben at the O2 Centre, on Finchley Road, in north London, just two days after I got out of rehab. Chi sensibly insisted that we drive round the car park a couple of times to check things out beforehand. Unknown to us, Ben was on his own but had already seen us and gone into the O2, where he called me to ask why I had this heavy-looking black guy with me. I assured him that he was just a friend and not there for any nasty stuff.

We arranged to meet at the bottom of some escalators inside the shopping centre. Eventually, Ben walked in with his hands in his pockets and I wondered if he was tooled up. He clearly had the hump with me.

I looked up and tried to smile in a relaxed manner. 'Hi.'

He just looked daggers back at me and then came right up close to me. 'You're comin' with me.'

Chi stepped between us and said, 'He ain't going nowhere.'

At this point, Ben was sticking his chest out a bit at my massive new 'friend' Chi.

'You're coming with me,' he repeated.

Clearly, Ben wanted to just take me away and lock me in his boot, but Chi was not going to let that happen. However, I knew I had to try to calm things down.

'Come on. Let's go and have a coffee and a chat. That's what we're here for.'

It was a tricky moment, because, if Ben decided to ignore me, I knew things would blow up even further. In the back of my mind was Chi's earlier advice; he'd said, if anything went wrong, he'd hold Ben back and I was to just leg it and get in a cab. 'I'll find you later,' Chi had explained in a remarkably calm voice.

But Ben agreed to go for a coffee, so we went upstairs and sat down and I tried to break it to Ben gently that I hadn't got any money for him.

Obviously, he wasn't happy. 'I fuckin' want my money ... what are you playin' at?'

Chi just sat there, observing it all without a saying a word.

'I can't pay you,' I said very apologetically. 'I am trying to sort it out but I can't do it right now.'

There was an eerie wall of silence between us after I said that.

Ben seemed to size things up. His eyes narrowed and I nervously waited for the next outburst. He took a deep breath and then said something (I can't remember the exact words) about how much I owed him, and then he mentioned a figure – '£200,000'.

I was astonished and said I thought it was much less than that. It's not so surprising that he got the hump with me after that. Then – out of nowhere – he took a swing at me right in the middle of that café.

Luckily, I saw it coming, ducked and he just missed me. Chi then grabbed Ben to try to stop it escalating. 'You gotta calm down,' said Chi. 'You gotta calm down.'

It was also bad news because we were obviously attracting a lot of attention in the busy shopping-centre café.

I realised that Ben was trying to prove a point. He was angry and he was fed up with me mucking him around. But, thank goodness, because of Chi's presence, he knew he wasn't going to achieve anything by being violent. After a couple of minutes of renewed calm, Ben said he'd give me a few weeks and then he walked off without another word.

Later that day, Ben called me and said, 'Listen, I want your and your wife's passports tonight. If you're not planning to run anywhere, then there's no reason for you to mind.'

I said, 'Fine.' After all, I thought to myself, I can easily go and get a new passport if I have to.

'Where do you want me to meet you?'

He said, 'Edgware … by the station.'

'I promise you I will be there.'

This was still just a couple of days after I'd got out of rehab.

That night, I went home and Nic got very, very angry when I told her we were going to give a complete stranger our passports. Hardly surprising, was it? I'd decided to tell her what had happened because I felt it was important to be honest with her as much as possible from now on.

Nic was insistent she didn't want to give up the passports. She was worried because they had photos of our kids, but I pointed out that was when they were babies. It really didn't matter. Eventually, she reluctantly agreed but she remained very upset. The truth is, neither of us had much choice in the matter.

So I met Ben and gave him the passports. I had to show good faith to him, otherwise he would probably have had me killed, with or without Chi in 'my corner'.

We were approaching Christmas 2007 and already rehab seemed a million years ago. Everything was back to the way it was. In fact, the dangers had increased. I was almost convinced that behind every corner another heavyweight criminal was hiding ready to put a bullet in my head over my so-called 'debts'.

OK – I had Chi with me most of the time now but I had to find the money to pay him. I needed to find a new source of cash again, and I also wanted to start earning some legitimate money as well.

Me, Nic and the kids were now living in another new, 'secret', rented home, well away from my old haunts. But the months after I got out of rehab were to turn into the worst period since all this mess first began.

There seemed to be no way to earn any legitimate money,

which meant borrowing more and more. Not only was I back in the hole, but I was getting deeper and deeper into it without any realistic means of escape. Everyone knew I was fucked, so a lot of people gave me a really wide berth. I even borrowed ten grand off a friend, which bought me a bit of time as we approached Christmas.

Desperate for legitimate work, some other characters started coming into my life as well. There was Yos, an Israeli jeweller from Chigwell. Initially, I had a meeting with him and his brother as I was still looking for investors for some new platinum deals. I acted as a broker for the buyer and seller. My commission would be 1 per cent. Most of the sellers were dealing in platinum as a way of collecting VAT as they were companies that owed VAT to the revenue people.

I then arranged a second meet with Yos one Sunday morning with some Indians, who'd driven down from Birmingham. They were a different mob of Indians from the previous lot. Yos was a very friendly, laidback character, and he knew I owed money all over the place but didn't seem bothered by it one bit. We all met up in an Israeli café in a park, in Hendon, because it was conveniently just off the M1. It was a friendly meeting because I didn't owe them any money – yet.

Yos's Indian 'mates' from Birmingham turned out to be run-of-the-mill jewellers and they were interested in putting some money up to trade in platinum. They immediately talked about £100,000, so that meant I could get my hands on £100,000, out of which I could give £50,000 to Ben to give myself some breathing space and then put the other £50,000 into the platinum to make myself some proper money.

Funnily enough, one of the Indians was called Ben as well. They wanted me to turn round money for them through these platinum deals. Now some people might call this a form of money laundering, but it's too easy to blame everything on 'money laundering', as it's the most overused expression, as far as I am concerned. This was 'business' in my mind. Nothing more, nothing less.

This is how it all worked. The platinum deals were supposed to end up with VAT owed to us. That means we brought platinum in from outside the UK into another English company, so we could legitimately claim the VAT.

At the end of each quarter, the VAT owed on £1 million, for example, would mean owing the VAT people £500,000, so that meant the VAT people had to pay the company back the other half. I was owed over £1 million from the VAT people, which would help the Indians' cash flow enormously. The carrot for me was I could earn 1 per cent commission for selling it.

Anyway, that was the theory. When I first met them, they didn't have a proper system in place, but they told me they would pay me £100,000 to buy platinum and then bring it into a British company. Besides using some of that money to pay back the other Ben, I also needed to pay Chi as my driver/protector, as well as keep my family going for a while with basic living expenses.

The Indians from Birmingham were meant to pay me that first £100,000 the following weekend, but this time the boot was on the other foot and they didn't turn up. The trouble was I had already promised Ben I would give him £25,000 and now I couldn't give it to him after all. Not good news.

Naturally, Ben started getting very vicious yet again. I'd been expecting trouble but I suppose I was hoping he might give up and fade away, although people like Ben tend not to do that. It started with more phone threats as he began really cranking up the pressure on me. I didn't really know what to do because I was still skint, but I didn't want him to know that, so I had to come up with something that would enable me to play for time.

Then I got a small 'break' of sorts. Ben wanted to buy a particular mobile phone for his daughter for Christmas and I had a contact who could get it, despite the fact it wasn't in the regular shops. So, when I told Ben this, he asked me to get him one. He also wanted a lady's Cartier watch.

He even said that, if I got him the watch and the phone, then it would take a bit of the pressure off me. I was all ears because I needed to play for time yet again. About a week before Christmas, I managed to get him the Cartier stainless steel watch and I also got him a £5,000 Breitling watch that he'd suddenly announced he also wanted with diamonds. I only charged him £2,000 for the Cartier watch, so he was a little bit happier with me … for the moment at least.

But then, a couple of days later, he was on my back for that mobile phone for his daughter as well. Trouble was, I couldn't get it anywhere. I knew I had to find one before Christmas or else I might end up 6ft under.

Eventually, I drove up to Tottenham Court Road and bought the mobile phone he wanted for £200. I then dropped it off at my mate Jerry's house so he could give it to Ben. This was supposed to give me some more breathing space on the debt so that I didn't have to cough up any money until just after Christmas.

Everything seemed calmer by the time I got home that evening, so we decided to have some sushi delivered to the house for all the family. It was a delicious meal and, for once in my life, I didn't keep checking my phone for irate messages and the atmosphere at home was better than it had been for months.

After we'd finished eating, I took all the sushi boxes and kitchen rubbish outside to the bin. It was 23 December 2007, and I remember it as icy cold outside that night, because I only had on a T-shirt and jeans and I was really shivering. I should have known what would happen next.

19
ROAD TO NOWHERE

Just as I was dropping the stuff in the bin, I heard a car horn go from the front of the house. I turned and looked into the darkness and there was Ben in a black BMW with another man.

Now I could have easily run back into the house and just ignored it. But, as you've probably already gathered, that's not my style. So I started walking over towards him to keep him away from the house. Ben jumped out of the BMW; he clearly wasn't a happy bunny.

'Jay … you're fuckin' takin' the piss, my son,' said Ben, his words turning into clouds of steam as he spoke. 'You're comin' for a ride with me.'

I tried to stay cool. 'Fine. No problem.'

I was hoping my calm, resigned response might throw him a bit. Then I asked him if I could get my jacket.

'No way, Jay. You gotta come in the car now.'

It didn't work but at least it was worth a try. I was prepared to do anything to prevent this psycho bunny from getting any closer to my family inside the house, so I shrugged my shoulders and just got in the car.

I knew Nic would be scared stiff about what had happened to me but *anything* was better than risking her and the children's lives.

As I clambered into the back of the BMW, I realised for the first time that the 'man' I thought was sitting in the front passenger seat was actually a girl in her twenties. At least that meant Ben was just passing when he decided to stop. That was good news in a sense because it meant he wasn't specifically 'gunning' for me, if you know what I mean.

But then, as we moved off into darkness, Ben made a call on his mobile. 'I've got him. He's in the car and he's on his own. Where shall we come to?'

Initially, the people he was talking to seemed a bit reluctant to answer Ben's question. It was a Saturday night after all, but Ben wouldn't let it go that easily. 'It's our fuckin' money and we need to deal with this fuckin' now. We are *not* lettin' it lie.'

The way he said '*not*' sent a shiver up my spine. We were on the North Circular Road by this time and I was seriously contemplating jumping out of the car.

The trouble was that all the lights were green and I would probably have been run over by the car behind if I got out when we were going at this speed. The girl in the front passenger seat didn't even look at me. I had no idea who she was.

Then I made a typical Jason move. I asked him a question that did not in any way relate to my current predicament. 'Did you get the phone I gave to Jerry?'

Ben didn't respond immediately. It felt as if he was trying to absorb the fact I had just come out of left field with a completely inane question in the middle of a kidnapping.

'Yeah … I got the fuckin' phone.' Then he unfortunately read my mind. 'And don't even think about fuckin' jumpin' out of the car because I'll catch you, yer cunt.'

I replied as calmly as I could, 'I'm not going anywhere, mate.'

So there I was thinking to myself I have no idea where this is going to end and whether I will live to see another day. Ben was on the phone most of the time but at least he wasn't always talking to people about me.

The black BMW eventually stopped in a busy street outside a station somewhere in Kilburn. This huge bloke appeared out of the shadows and suddenly ripped open the passenger door next to me and squeezed in. I had to shuffle across the seat sharpish.

I was just settling into the other side of the back seat when an almost identical bloke to the first one got in next to me as well. I was now crammed in the back of a five series BMW between two massive lumps of muscle. And both their faces were disguised by jumpers that covered the bottom half of their faces, complete with hoods and huge, thick puffa jackets that filled up even more of the back of that BMW. I could hardly breathe. It all seemed very worrying.

Just then the girl got out and yet another heavy clambered into the front passenger seat. This was looking very ominous. All I recall about these blokes was that they were all white.

Then the one in the front started on me. 'You cunt. You've had my money, yer cunt. Yer fuckin' cunt.'

Then it was more 'cunt … cunt … cunt' stuff. Obviously, I was bricking it. I didn't say a word. Somehow, I managed to make myself stay calm. It was almost a feeling of resigned indifference.

In the back of my mind, I was thinking to myself they weren't going to do anything to me because they wanted their money. If they killed me, then that would be the end of that and they would all be out of pocket.

It didn't make sense. I kept telling myself, 'This is all a warning.' But then another little voice kept saying over the top of everything else, 'Don't kid yourself, Jason … These blokes mean business.'

Suddenly, the BMW took off and did a sharp left-hand swerve into a much darker side road. Then we pulled over again and this time they all started shouting at me. 'Where is our fuckin' money?'

I must have shrunk even more in size between those two lumps in their vast puffa jackets in the back seat of the BMW. I was crammed between them and I knew I had to come up with something very quickly.

So I told them a load of platinum stock had just been delivered to the refinery at Tilbury. I knew it was closed at weekends so hopefully that would give me some breathing space. I told them it was shut until 27 December. Naturally, I'd made it all up. Then I said in a very chirpy, relaxed manner, 'If you pick me up that morning, we can go to the refinery and you can pick all your stuff up.'

More silence followed as their not very big brains absorbed what I had said. I was encouraged because at least they hadn't whacked me with a cosh or something for suggesting we reconvene after Christmas.

I am convinced to this day they were seriously contemplating letting me go at that moment but then the one in the front sadly came up with a scheme. 'We're going to lock you up in a warehouse over Christmas and then we'll take you there when the refinery is open.'

I tried to respond as 'normally' as possible. 'If you do that, then my wife will call the police. She's probably already done that anyway. I haven't even told her I've gone out and, if I call her and say everything's OK but I am not going to be back until 27 December, then she won't believe me. Listen … I'll go and do whatever you want me to do, but you have to think about what you're saying.'

I sat there waiting for an explosion when the strangest thing happened; my 'protector' Chi just happened to drive right past the BMW in his Range Rover. I was astounded.

I didn't say a word but then Ben spotted Chi's car and said, 'What the fuck is he doing round here?'

I said, 'I dunno.' And it was the truth.

Obviously, they were all wondering if he'd been watching everything all along. They started saying things like, 'We'll do that black bastard if we have to.'

But I knew when I'd watched Chi drive past that he hadn't even seen us. It had to be a coincidence. Not surprisingly, they instantly became very jumpy.

'Don't involve anyone else in this, OK?' one of them said. 'It's our fuckin' money. Don't involve any other cunts in our money.'

I nodded my head, anxious to keep them calm but realising that maybe Chi's accidental appearance was not such good news, because it had made them much more agitated. I started thinking that one of these clowns either side of me would stick a knife in me sooner rather than later.

A wall of silence enveloped the car and it was very eerie. I just kept waiting and waiting for something to happen. I counted down the seconds of silence in my head for some-thing to do because I needed some sort of diversion to avoid wetting myself.

Then suddenly – about five minutes after Chi had disappeared – they announced they were getting out of the car 'for a chat'. The two in the back demanded all my phones off me but, of course, I didn't have any. But I was mightily relieved that at last I could breathe properly once they got out.

They then stood a few yards away from the car in a huddle. God knows what they were discussing but it was a safe bet it was something to do with me. I thought for a moment about making a run for it but then I changed my mind. Maybe nothing bad would happen? Typical of me. The eternal bloody optimist up to his usual old tricks again.

Then all three got back in the BMW, and the one in the front passenger seat turned to me and said, 'This is what's goin' to happen now, you fuckin' piece of shit.'

God knows why, but I tried to smile in his direction at that moment.

He paused while the two lumps either side of me nodded in agreement, their puffa jackets rustling in a very sinister manner.

Then the one in front continued, 'We are taking you home and you have to give us your mobile phones – *all* of them – and your laptop because we don't want you to have any communication with people.'

'OK,' I replied.

Was that it? I couldn't quite believe my ears.

Then Ben started up the BMW and we headed off back towards the North Circular. As we progressed through north London, the three lumps got out at different places and in the end it was just Ben and me.

I did wonder for a few moments if perhaps they'd deliberately lulled me into a false sense of security and now Ben was going to sort me out. But I just kept quiet in the back seat.

The trouble was, I didn't want Ben to take me to my house, so about a couple of miles away from my place I said, 'You know the police will be there.'

'What do you mean?' asked Ben.

'Well, I've gone and thrown the rubbish out and haven't come back for hours.' I felt like adding, 'It's bleedin' obvious, you fuckin' idiot.' But I kept quiet while he thought about what I had just said.

After another couple of minutes' silence, I had to speak. It's one of my weaknesses, as you have no doubt noticed. I don't like long, awkward silences and this was in danger of turning into one of those.

'I don't want you to get nicked,' I said. 'Neither of us needs that sort of aggravation. If the cops are there, I'll make out I've just been out for a ride with a friend, but it'd be better if they didn't see you, don't you think?'

At that moment, Ben suddenly pulled the BMW over next to a phone box and turned towards me in the back seat. 'Right. Go and phone your house and see if the cops have been called.'

Moments later, I was ringing home. 'Hi, Nic, it's me … have you called the police?'

But then Ben grabbed the phone off me and demanded an answer. Luckily, Nic – bless her – remained very calm and insisted, 'No, I didn't call the police.'

It was the opposite of what I wanted her to say, so, after putting the phone down, I said to Ben, 'I don't believe her. I think she has called them.'

God knows where I got all this courage from. Call it survival instinct or something – probably a dose of terror-fuelled adrenalin – was keeping me going.

Obviously, I didn't want Ben anywhere near my house; I preferred him to drop me off somewhere and for me to make my own way home. But he clearly had other ideas. Then, as we got within 200 yards of my house, I saw my parents' car outside.

There was no way I wanted to involve my family in all this. Just then, Ben turned the corner and went down the street alongside my house and stopped next to another telephone box.

'We don't want our faces to be known, so you call your wife and tell her to get your five mobile phones and your laptop and walk them down to the bus stop at the end of your road and leave them in a bag there.'

I was completely dumfounded by Ben's request, because I had forgotten for the moment about his earlier demands for the phones and computers. I should have seen it coming, though, because it made complete and utter sense.

So I phoned Nic and assured her nothing bad would happen and that she just needed to stay calm. I told her where to take the bag with the computer and mobile phones. But I didn't want them to have them all, so I told her about some old phones, knowing full well that it meant I would be left with a couple of useable ones.

Anyway, she got them all together and we watched from the car as she dropped the bag by the bus stop. Before picking them up, we drove past the house again and suddenly, out of nowhere, a police car appeared.

Ben turned angrily towards me and ordered me to put my head down. I reluctantly did as I was told because I knew he'd probably blow my head off if I didn't comply.

After the police car had gone, Ben dropped me off 200 yards from the house. I went and picked up the bag and ran it over to him in the car. He checked the contents and then waved me away.

I then walked straight to the house. Nic and my mum and dad

looked horrified when they opened the front door. They examined me to see if I had been hurt and my dad gave me a medicinal nip of brandy to calm my nerves. I couldn't quite believe that I was back at home unscathed after a tour of north London in the company of a bunch of psychotic gangsters.

After knocking back that brandy, I phoned my 'protector' Chi and asked him to get round to my place right away. That's when he said he was already outside. I was confused and frankly a little suspicious. What was going on? First of all he drives past me in Kilburn, and now he is hanging around near my house.

Then it emerged that, when I was first ordered to get into Ben's BMW hours earlier, our dog had started barking and that had prompted Nicole to look out of the front door where she saw me being driven off. She even noticed half the number plate and had said it was a red BMW when it was black, but at least she tried!

Anyway, Nic then phoned Chi and he asked her if my phone was still in the house, which it was. He then told her to find a number for Ben because he had a feeling it was him who'd turned up outside my house that night. But Ben's phone didn't pick up and I actually remembered him ignoring some calls when we were in the BMW earlier. Then my mum and dad came over and they called the police.

Because I was 'known' to the local constabulary, the police sent two detectives around who interviewed my mum and dad separately because they were highly suspicious about the whole 'incident'.

As Nic was telling me all this, I heard Chi roll up outside so I popped outside and jumped into his Range Rover for a chat.

Chi was outraged by what had happened and told me, 'They have taken this to a different level now. We need to get this all sorted out.' I wasn't so sure I wanted this to go any further.

I knew I had until 27 December to save my skin but I also knew we had to move out of the house as soon as possible because Ben would inevitably be back soon. We stayed at the house that night because it was too late to make other arrangements.

Then early the next morning, we went to a friend's house for the day and then on to the Hendon Hall Hotel, where England's 1966 World Cup-winners stayed. We took a family suite for two nights and, on Christmas Day, we moved to a hotel in Chelsea where we stayed until Boxing Day. I knew only too well that the following day – 27th – the shit would really hit the fan.

It was like a ticking time-bomb over that Christmas period. I hoped I might be able to pull off that £100,000 platinum deal, which could just buy me some time, but it was unlikely to materialise over the holiday period.

On Boxing Day, we took the kids ice skating and did a lot of family things together. It felt like the right thing to do because I knew only too well that, the following day, I might never see my family again. Also, by being out and about, I knew it would be harder for them to find me.

20
LIAR, LIAR

Just after I'd woken up on what I really thought might just prove to be the last day of my life – 27 December – I got a call from the police who wanted to see me. I was actually very relieved because this might give me some 'cover' to avoid the inevitable onslaught.

The police said they'd been looking into that 'kidnap' incident involving Ben after my dad had called them in, and they told me they'd been to the registered owner of the BMW and he turned out to be a friend of Ben's, a banker. I'd actually met this guy quite a few times. The police visited this bloke and he told them his friend Ben had been using the car at that time. The police then warned this guy that, if anyone went near me, they'd get nicked.

The police then said they wanted to see me at my house 'urgently'. I hadn't wanted to go back there ever again after what had happened, but they assured me they'd have the police outside to keep an eye on things.

So Nic and I went back to the house and we were interviewed by two detectives. At least this would help me play for a bit of time. I also knew my main protector Henry was away on holiday until early January, and I didn't want to do anything until he came back. I told the police the story I'd concocted in Ben's car – that a friend of mine had pulled up and taken me for a drive to visit a couple of his friends and it was all a misunderstanding.

One of the detectives got very angry then and said, 'That's complete bollocks. Why are you lying?'

'I am not lying,' I replied. 'I do owe these people money and once I pay them then that's the end of it.'

The cops weren't particularly satisfied with my answer but they had no choice in the matter. They also advised me not to stay at the house, but I'd already made that decision for myself and my family's sake. They insisted they'd have a police car outside but I knew that wouldn't help much.

So we packed some more stuff up and went to stay in a hotel in the New Forest until New Year's Day. The police presence outside the house did at least stop anyone coming near us because it was clear the long arm of the law was now involved. And the one good thing about them taking all my phones off me was that they couldn't expect me to call them but, then again, I knew they'd find me soon.

Of course, I'd got myself another pay-as-you-go phone but I wasn't planning to call Ben and all my other creditors for a chat.

At least having everything swiped off me had certain advantages. Luckily, we got a great deal at the hotel and my dad kindly paid for it on his credit card. We even bumped into some old school friends, so, all in all – considering I'd been close to death a few days earlier – we had a very nice time. But I knew all this peace and quiet wouldn't last long.

On 2 January 2008, I got the call I was praying for from one of the Indians in Birmingham to say they had my payment for the first platinum deal. They said it was about £120,000. I was so relieved. I decided to drive straight up to Birmingham to get it.

I was in a friend's Land Rover Discovery at the time and I had to meet one of the Indians in a service station on the motorway. We met up and I went to the boot of his car and he said there was £80,000 in there. I was disappointed and said I thought there was going to be more. He assured me there would be more later in the week, so I just said, 'Fine,' and headed off back down the motorway.

At least I now had some cash to use to keep people off my back for a few days. Having that money also allowed me to relax enough to realise that I had to get tougher with these people and try to resolve all these problems properly, not keep running away from everything.

I knew Henry was about to get back from his holiday and I believed he was the key to my long-term survival. But I owed Henry some money, so I gave it to him and bunged him another grand to get in touch with everyone else on my behalf. He agreed to 'represent' me fully. It was a major breakthrough for me because I could no longer commit to paying Chi two grand a week as I simply wasn't earning it. In any case, Henry was far more 'effective'.

When one heavyweight villain came on the phone trying to give it double large, Henry just got on the line and this guy completely changed his tune. Henry was respected by all of them and that was the key in his 'game'. He didn't want to hurt anyone. He liked the fact that he could get what he wanted through his reputation alone, most of the time.

I gave Henry £65,000 to give to Ben after the Birmingham platinum Indians paid the rest of that first payment. That bought me a bit of time, although one of the guys in Birmingham made a point of letting me know he was friendly with one of the members of that notorious crime family. In other words, don't fuck with us. Now I had another member of Britain's most powerful crime family on my back.

So, by getting much more involved in the heavier side of things through Henry, I was taking everything to another level – a more criminal level. What really sums up the hole I was in was that I went back up to Birmingham with £8,000 in interest for the Indians and gave it to them out of their own money. Robbing Peter to pay Paul, as I have so often described it.

Then the Indians 'invested' another £100,000. Isn't that complete madness? Talk about juggling. Everything was getting very tight and claustrophobic again. But at least Henry kept Ben away from me and eventually we were even able to move back into our house.

And, of course, in the middle of all this, I continued hustling for legitimate business. I got a call from a financier who claimed to have someone who wanted to buy some gold. It sounded like a deal that might really get me out of the shit.

I still occasionally used Chi as my driver when Henry was not available, so I took him to a meeting with two Essex gangsters called Tom and Peter plus an old boy called Anthony. Peter looked like a boxer and Tom looked like a terrorist.

They turned up in Range Rovers like typical Essex gangsters. They were obsessed with talking about the gold.

The old boy Anthony started banging on about how he could get gold worth £1 million a month out of Peru. That meant I stood to earn around £200,000 a month out of it, if it really was possible. But, once again, I was stupidly and desperately pinning my hopes on a deal that was nothing more than hot air at this stage. It was only then it dawned on me that Anthony and the other two hoods had only come to me because I had access to a refinery and my dad was an old-time jeweller.

But, for the moment, the gold deal seemed to be real, and every morning I'd get emails with contracts to sign. But nothing was actually happening in reality. We even had a lawyer from Peru who'd gone back out there to set everything up. This guy claimed he'd seen the gold in Peru and I got a call saying he was flying it back and that the 'product' would be in London the following Monday. So I arranged to meet Anthony – who was basically the middleman – and his partner and the South American lawyer so we could then arrange to transfer it to the refinery.

Within minutes of getting to the hotel for the meet, the lawyer dangled some keys under my nose and told me they belonged to the boxes of gold, 'which are still in Peru'. I was suspicious.

The lawyer insisted on showing us photos of the gold in Peru but it didn't mean anything. It all sounded so dodgy. They'd even paid £250,000 for export duty. Peter and Tom remained convinced the deal was still happening. They even shelled out £50,000 to me to put into some other deals, as if to prove to me they believed the Peruvian gold was on its way. They presumed I'd make them more money but that £50,000 went straight to Birmingham to pay back some of the money I owed that lot. The cycle was in full flow and I was the only one who was going to come out poorer in the long run.

It was now March 2008 and I knew I only had a few weeks left until Easter to pay Ben more of his money, otherwise he'd come after me all over again. Good old Henry then bought me a bit more time by flexing his muscles. He was proving as good as gold, if you'll excuse the pun.

But I was still sliding back to where I was in terms of trouble at an alarming rate, although I was kidding myself into thinking it wasn't as bad as before. I was managing to sell a few watches but no way was I earning enough money to cover all my debt payments. I knew I was going to have to get another loan, sooner rather than later.

I managed to pay back the best part of £100,000 to the Indians in Birmingham but they were expecting everything to be paid off by April at the latest. My parents knew it wasn't looking good for me but they believed that, with Henry behind me, I was much safer than before. It was certainly true that I was more protected. But I didn't let my father know just how much was going on because I didn't want to worry him after all he'd been through in recent years.

So I got to Easter 2008 and Henry gave me some friendly advice: 'Jason, why don't you fuck off for a while because all these characters are going to be hunting you down soon, my old mate.' Henry was good for really useful advice from time to time, and perhaps if I'd taken one of his favourite sayings more to heart, I wouldn't have found myself in quite so much shit. He told me, 'You can't be wrong and strong.'

The Birmingham people and Ben were the biggest risks to my health because I still owed them £200,000 each; then there was £50,000 to a guy called Frank and his people; not to mention the interest repayments of 10 per cent a month. It was one hell of debt mountain to climb.

So I took Henry's advice and we left the house, knowing full well that certain people would be paying me a visit, sooner rather than later. I had already booked a holiday to the States for the following Christmas, so I pushed that forward to Easter, enabling us to get away immediately.

I still hadn't completely paid for the holiday a few days before we were due to depart and we still didn't have our passports because we'd handed them over to Ben months earlier after that kidnapping business. So we had to apply for new ones and pretend they'd been stolen.

The day before we were about to go, I paid a cheque for the

remainder of the cost of the holiday, knowing full well that it wouldn't bounce until I arrived in the States. I'd booked Club class tickets and all the best hotels and owed the agent about £17,000 for this holiday but, amazingly, he accepted the cheque. You may be thinking, why did I book such an expensive holiday? It's simple – you only get credit with top-of-the-range holidays. There is no way you can book a Thomas Cook holiday and give a cheque the day before you leave. I also thought the Anthony deal would happen while I was away and all the bills would be sorted.

Obviously, I didn't want anyone to know where we were going. We went to Chicago first to visit a friend. Minutes after landing, I got a message on my answerphone from Ben saying I had a couple of weeks left and then that was it. It wasn't exactly a nice way to arrive in paradise.

With platinum continuing to arrive every day in London, I even took my laptop with me to the States so I could do my invoices while I was on holiday. Everything seemed to be going as smooth as velvet. For the first time in years and years, I seemed to be gradually getting out of that bloody financial hole.

But I should have known better. While I was away, I was raided by the VAT people and the bloke who was paying me my commission on behalf of the platinum guys suddenly got cold feet. He and the Greeks were convinced the raid was connected to me and that, now I was under observation, he wanted to put the brakes on all the deals for a month.

This was disastrous news for me. I tried to talk them out of it on the phone from the States. I arrived back from Florida on a Monday morning and drove straight round to see the main link man to the Greeks. He'd just agreed to do a £4 million deal with the Greeks and they were sitting on the stock and I had to stop the delivery of it. I said I'd sort it out within a couple of days but this character would not allow me back into the deal and he even told the Greeks he couldn't risk upsetting the Revenue people. It was a disaster.

I tried to assure the Greeks it would all be fine and suggested putting that deal through my dad's company and he'd then sell it on to another guy, which would get round the problem with the VAT people. But it didn't work out so I had to sell it to someone else.

I was also doing another platinum deal with a bloke in Dubai. But it ended up just being one big deal worth a couple of million. After that, they said they didn't want any more stock from me. For the first time in years, I had actually been earning money with ease and now something had happened which was completely out of my control.

By September 2008, I owed the Greeks almost £230,000 because the money had been held up after we tried to push it through my dad. By the time we finally got the money across to the Greeks, they claimed they'd lost £350,000 because the price of platinum had plummeted, plus £90,000 worth of currency exchange differential because it had dropped during the delay in selling.

Typically, I tried to put some happy spin on it by saying there would be more money coming, but then I began panicking and started stupidly sending them fraudulent bits of paper to keep them off my back. It was suicidal on my part because I was saying I had sent money when I hadn't. How stupid could I be?

I hadn't even told Henry about my latest 'problem'. Then I got a call from the Greeks to go and see them. I presumed it was going to be a heavy meeting.

When my mate Lucas decided at the last moment he didn't want an expensive Patek Philippe watch I'd got for him, I offered it to the Greeks when I met them at the Grove Hotel, near Watford. 'That's a present for you,' I told the main man.

He looked surprised and, of course, it was just a way to fob him off really. But at least he seemed sympathetic, saying, 'Come on, Jay. You gotta start payin' some dough. You can't just leave it hangin'.'

I said, 'No, no ... It'll be all right. We'll get trading again and everything will be OK.'

At least by giving him that expensive watch I had thrown him something to help avoid being taken to the cleaners there and then.

After that meeting, I managed to delay the Greeks for weeks until I got another, much heavier call: 'Jay, we gotta sort this out. Lay your cards on the table. Come down and see me.'

I knew that meant trouble.

21

BEWARE GREEKS BEARING FISTS

I really had no choice but to enter the lion's den – literally. I convinced myself the Greeks wouldn't do anything to me at their office, but, if I am to be honest about it, I was tired and fed up by this stage. In some ways, I was starting not to care. I felt so worn down by everything.

So I drove down to the Greeks' office in Enfield. Seconds after parking up, I noticed the main man, to whom I'd earlier given the watch, in the big boardroom as I began walking up the stairs to his reception. He was talking to loads of people who were gathered round him. His secretary sent me up to a smaller office on the floor above. I remember when I got up there looking down at the ground three storeys below and wondering if anyone had ever been thrown out of there.

As I waited, a belt of tension gripped me. I wondered what was going to happen next. In one sense, I was resigned to it, but I couldn't help asking myself why I'd chosen to put myself in danger. Finally, the main man walked in with a cheery smile on his face and said, 'What's happening, Jay? Have you got me any money?'

It was a clever approach because it threw me. I was expecting a headlong rush into aggression, but he seemed positively happy and relaxed, so I tried to match him.

'Yeah. Some more money has arrived in my bank account but it hasn't cleared yet.'

'Fair enough. I'm just finishing up this meeting and I'll be back in a minute.'

With that, he disappeared again. I couldn't quite believe my ears. This seemed to be going much better than expected. I looked through the window of the small office I was standing in, to where some of the men and women worked in that much bigger, open-plan office.

Something about the way one or two of them glanced knowingly at me set a little alarm bell ringing in my head but I pushed it to the back of my mind for the moment.

Just then, he walked back into the office with these two huge, fucking pieces of Greek muscle who could barely fit through the doorway. This time, the main man wasn't smiling. 'You know why they are here, don't you?'

'No, not really,' I said nervously.

Then he turned and pointed towards one of the lumps. 'You owe this geezer £350,000.'

As he said that, I thought to myself (not for the first time in my life), 'Fuck me!'

Then I said, 'I've already paid some money. I don't owe £350,000.'

One or two beats of silence followed. I didn't know how to react next.

Then, out of nowhere, the main man hit me very hard across my face with the back of his hand. I've never forgotten it because it was the first time I'd ever been hit in my entire life. I remember my head just snapped to the side and all this blood spurted over my shirt. I didn't even realise it was mine at first; I just looked down at it in surprise.

I'd had a lot of sinus operations in the past so I guess my nose was the worst place to get hit. Soon the blood was spurting everywhere out of my nose and then I said the bleeding (sorry) obvious: 'Please get me some tissues.'

He passed me a box from the top of the desk in front of me. It was odd how he had them there for just such an 'emergency'.

The men and women in the open-plan office must have seen everything but the main man didn't seem to care one bit. After all, he was the boss so he could do whatever he wanted. He looked at me then with a definite touch of venom in his eyes, and began shouting, 'How are you going to pay us? How are you going to fuckin' pay us?'

I then went into classic Jason defensive mode. 'I can pay ... I can pay.'

Then he said, 'Empty your pockets.'

I didn't respond immediately because I was confused.

'Empty your fuckin' pockets.'

I put my wallet on the desk in front of him. He pulled out my Connect card, which would provide access to my cash.

'How much money is in there?'

I knew the one thing I couldn't do was lie about it, because they could just get me to go to a bank and then they'd know, so I decided to tell the truth for a change. 'There's £27,000 on there.'

The main man didn't say a word in response but just walked out of the open door of the office and handed the card to a girl at a desk in the adjoining, open-plan office. She pulled out a card machine and he told her, 'Take £27,000 off that.'

I had to punch out the code but it wouldn't go through. The main man grimaced at me and the girl tried again. The tension was building up because I knew that, if this card didn't work, he would probably throw me out of that window as he'd clearly had enough of my bullshit.

I took a gamble then and interrupted the girl as she started to try to re-enter the card details. 'I'll phone the bank and make sure they authorise it.'

The three lumps raised their eyebrows in surprise at my attitude but I was battling to save my life here so there was no time for trickery. They handed me the phone and I went through a series of card security questions and within a few minutes the £27,000 had been authorised. But that wasn't enough for these characters.

'Give us your full name and the address of where you are living and write it all down. We will know if you are lying, so don't bother.'

Then one of the two Greek lumps chipped in, 'You fuckin' can't hide behind anyone,' which was then repeated by his mate. In other words, they were implying that I couldn't get Henry involved. And throughout all this there was blood still pouring out of my nose and I was struggling to soak it all up with their tissues, mainly because I'd just stuffed the last of them over my nose.

Soon the blood was seeping through my hands from my nose. Not a pleasant sight. One of them walked out of the office into a side room and then came straight back with a loo roll, which he gave to me without uttering a word.

'Thanks,' I said, trying not to sound bitter in case they decided to hit me again just for the hell of it.

At least I'd got through this in one piece, I thought to myself. But I wasn't home and dry yet.

I made a move to leave the room and that's when one of them picked up a baseball bat and slapped it in the palm of his hand over and over again. 'So you're going to pay this money, aren't you? We don't want to involve your family in this.'

I said, 'Listen, guys, I came to this office voluntarily. No one forced me to come here. I want to sort all this out.'

The main man said, 'Fair enough.'

'We want that £90,000 sorted out and then that £350,000.'

'Yeah … yeah. It will be done.'

I knew the £350,000 was bollocks but I wasn't about to argue with them.

'You can go now.'

I was still shitting myself because I'd spotted this white van rolling into the car park downstairs while we were in the office. I was convinced they were going to throw me in the back of it and dump me in the river with some concrete shoes. I was eventually 'escorted' down the stairs to the car park by the two lumps and told I had two weeks to sort out the £350,000. I kept looking at the white van for any sign of activity.

It was pitch-dark by this time and the office was at the end of a cul de sac. Not a great place to be feeling vulnerable. Once downstairs, I was left by my escorts and knew I now had to turn right into an even darker car park. I hesitated because it felt as if I was walking into a trap. So I turned left instead and walked towards the street because I thought I was going to get a kicking in the car park. I didn't care about my car.

Just then, one of the lumps shouted at me as I was walking the wrong way. 'Hey, mate, your car's over there.'

I thought to myself, 'Oh shit. They're really going to do me.'

I looked over at them and they were both grinning ear to ear. I swallowed hard and stopped for a moment. Then I turned around and headed for my Jag as fast as possible. I had blood all over my face. I was very shaky but I just wanted to get the fuck out of there.

I kept a close eye on that white van as I got to the Jag. My hands were shaking so badly I could barely get the key in the lock. And all the time I could feel those two lumps watching me from the office.

I've never felt so relieved as when I turned that key and the engine sparked into life. Once I got out on to the main road, I suddenly remembered I was supposed to pick my kids up from swimming lessons at 6.00pm that night. I looked at my watch and it was a quarter-to-six. Shit! I hated letting my family down but I could hardly turn up at the swimming pool with blood all over me and expect no one to notice.

So I rang Nic and said very calmly, 'I've been delayed. Can you pick the kids up?'

There were so many similar 'crossovers' between my so-called normal life and the world I had become embroiled in because of my massive debts. I was normally very good at covering up the crossovers. No matter how much shit I was in, I'd nearly always get home and greet my wife and family with a smile. Yet only moments earlier, I might have been on the phone in the driveway being informed that, if I didn't pay up, some thug was going to come over and pull my eyes out. It was a strain putting on this façade but it felt like the only way to keep going.

While Nic was out picking up the kids, I arrived home, took my shirt off and tidied myself up before they all returned. When I heard Nic's car outside, I came out of the house to greet them all. I was so relieved to be back with my family.

Obviously, Nic noticed something was wrong the moment she saw my swollen nose, so I told her what had happened and showed her my shirt. She was horrified. Remember, that was the first act of violence I had ever suffered. I was also worried they might come back to the house that night. I didn't sleep a wink. But at least Nic wasn't angry this time because she knew I hadn't done anything wrong, unlike previously. And they didn't come back, thank God.

Just before the end of 2008, I also borrowed £70,000 off a car-dealer mate of Lucas's called Lee Downs, the godfather to Lucas's kids. I needed some money to sort out the Greeks and the Dubai people. He was a short south Londoner who was certainly no mug when it came to business. He had a large car repair garage and a huge property portfolio. Lee had clearly been on both sides of the dock and he knew exactly who to call when he needed any heavy 'help'. But, despite all that, he was a perfectly friendly bloke as long as you didn't cross him.

The following day, I went to see my 'protector' Henry, despite the warnings from that Greek lot in Enfield not to involve him. Henry immediately told me never to go to meetings like that again. He actually had a bit of a go at me, but he was right – I shouldn't have walked into that place on my own. I'd been asking for trouble.

Then he phoned them and insisted on another meeting and they took notice when Henry spoke. So we had this meeting in Hertfordshire and they agreed I didn't owe them as much as £350,000 – they dropped their demands to a much more manageable £60,000! I wasn't even included in the conversation. They reckoned the depreciation of platinum prices was all my fault, but the way they 'recalculated' their figures summed it all up. What a stitch -up!

Then, finally, one of them turned to me and said, 'So, how are you going to pay the £60,000, Jay?'

I said, 'Well, the only way I can pay the £60,000 is by working for you guys to pay it off.'

'No, no, no. We're not doing that,' they said.

'Then I can offer you five grand a month. There's nothing else I can do.'

So, to make the payments, I had to find other sources of income – and, while I should have been able to earn enough to keep my head above water through my platinum deals, a mixture of bad luck and my old habits came back to haunt me. Nothing was ever straightforward where I was concerned.

As I mentioned earlier, I had this deal running with these people from Dubai and I was paying this guy a ½ per cent of my 1 per cent every month. I'd meet him in the West End and, as long as he got his five or six grand on time, he was very happy. The Dubai deal meant I was still earning a little money but it wasn't up to the levels it should have been. But at least, while I had some money coming in the door, it gave me a chance of survival.

But the Dubai deal stopped in November 2008 when I still seemed to owe them £200 000, which was down to the currency problem yet again. Then I started doing the old fraud routine again by making up bits of paper to show I had sent money when I hadn't.

So, I was soon up to my old tricks once more, which was really fucking stupid of me. I was back-pedalling like crazy. I had to find money for the Greeks and now this lot and I was really suffering in my head because just a few months earlier I'd seemed to be getting my life in order. But now it had started falling apart all over again.

The Dubai deal had come via a bloke who was an Indian mate of my friend Dave. This guy had a severe 'small man' syndrome. He was obsessed with platinum and was forever trying to get me to set up deals. He never went anywhere without his 6ft minder, a hunky, film star-looking type, who actually turned out to be as sharp as a pin. Gangsters who lived in Dubai called it 'living in the sand' and there were more and more of them doing it.

And that's when I started getting nasty phone calls from the Indians in Dubai. 'Listen to us, you Jew cunt.' The Indians always seem to call me 'Jew cunt'. 'We fuckin' know people in London who are going to fuckin' smash you up.' And so it went on. I'm sure you get the picture.

I kept going to Henry with all these problems but there was only so much he could do to sort them out. Ultimately, I had to take responsibility for my own mess. But Henry still remained very valuable to me. After that nasty call from the Indians in Dubai, I got him to phone them up and say he was working with me, and it did the trick because they calmed right down.

But the Indians didn't stay away for long. In December 2008, this same guy came back from Dubai and got straight in his car and drove down from Manchester to see me. I told him that the stock had been held up at a refinery in Acton but, of course, that was all a lie.

I decided to take my pal Dave because he had connections with the Dubai lot and I needed some back-up since Henry wasn't around. I had been told this Dubai guy was coming on his own and he said he'd be at junction 10 on the M1. Then he changed it to junction 11 and I realised none of it was stacking up properly. He was undoubtedly waiting for someone else to arrive as his 'back-up'. That meant he was planning something.

22

SPINNING PLATES

As we drove in convoy for the meeting, with Dave in his Range Rover and me in my car, I noticed there was this massive black geezer following behind the Dubai contact in another car. I freaked out because I could see they were up to something, so I drove off. He saw me pulling away and rang on my mobile. 'You're going to make this worse for yourself, I can tell you.'

He convinced me to turn round and have a proper meeting in the car park. I actually managed to get them to sit in my car. I don't know why I did that because it still meant they could have stabbed me or worse.

The big black bloke and this lairy Indian bastard both sat behind me, while Dave was next to me. I was in the driving seat. The Indian guy then said, 'What's going on then?' The big black bloke said nothing.

I told them that their £200,000 worth of platinum was at the refinery, called CARGO.

One of them said, 'If we phone CARGO now, will they will confirm it is there?'

I replied, 'Well, no, because I can't phone them as it's after 3.00pm and they don't answer the phone then.'

But they ignored me and rang CARGO anyway. I was shitting myself. This guy convinced CARGO he was speaking on behalf of a legitimate company and then the woman in the office said she could confirm there was a consignment of platinum there. I was astonished; it was a huge slice of luck.

Satisfied that I wasn't lying, this bloke then got his calculator out and worked out the exact amount they thought they had at CARGO, which, of course, I had lied about. After that, they were much nicer to me and let me out of the car convinced that things would be resolved in the next few days. I was very relieved.

Obviously, they'd find out soon enough that I'd lied, but by then I'd refuse to go to any more meetings with them. Henry would hopefully hold them back and luckily they didn't know where I lived.

I got more calls from other creditors over Christmas. It seemed like I couldn't get any rest from these people at all but I had to keep going somehow. This was my life now – chaos.

So, by the end of 2008, things had clearly taken yet another turn for the worse. The Indians kept that pressure on me right the way through the Christmas break and into the New Year. It was relentless and it was putting enormous strain on every aspect of my life.

The only way out seemed to be to find a new source of finance, however mad that must sound. Getting a new person to borrow money from was fundamental to my survival because I knew I could do nothing to stop my borrowing going on to another level in order to survive.

But this time I'd decided to steer clear of gangster loan sharks and managed to find one of the dads – I'll call him 'Steven' – at my kids' school to lend me money. It just shows how potty and desperate I had become. This was the ultimate crossover between my private life and my so-called 'business' world. I had tried so hard to avoid doing this in the past, but here I was doing it anyway.

We'd been out for dinner a couple of times and Steven liked talking business more than anything else. And he knew full well I was buying and selling platinum, so one day he just called me out of the blue and said he wanted to come in on a deal.

I told Steven I had the perfect deal for him because someone had just pulled out, meaning he could buy himself into it. I said it involved about £400,000 worth of platinum. That seemed to hook him in because he called back the next day and said he definitely wanted to do that deal.

He said he couldn't pay the full amount until the end of January but he sent me £100,000 as a deposit, which naturally I then used to buy some time with some of my other creditors. Going round and round in circles was my only chance. I was taking yet more risks, but what else could I do?

I knew more money was coming from Steven so I told the heaviest creditors, 'If you don't get the money by 31 January, do what you want to me.'

Amazingly, that response seemed to buy me a bit of time. Then Steven – who was supposed to send me the outstanding balance – went completely quiet on me, which was very worrying. It was only three or four days before the money was due to everyone else and I couldn't even track him down. I knew that, if I failed to make certain payments this time, I really might end up 6ft under.

Eventually, I called Steven's wife and said I was very worried because he'd disappeared. She assured me he was in New York on business. Two minutes after I'd put the phone down on her, the man himself called me and said he was a bit short but he would give me the money so long as I could guarantee he'd get it back within a week. Naturally, I promised him I would. The truth was I was so desperate for it I would have said he'd get it back within an hour.

By this time in early 2009, I needed to find more than half-a-million quid, even though I'd got rid of some of my heavier creditors the previous year.

Throughout all these problems, Lucas loyally remained my friend, even though he was another creditor, so I went out of my way to try to pay him back all his money. So I needed more than £500,000 to kick-start 2009 and wipe the slate clean and start to try to sort out my life.

Then all the money came through by the end of January from Steven. It was a massive relief because it meant I could maybe start to get rid of the Dubai people and others. I even managed to keep back a little bit of money to pay for rent and stuff like that.

The only slight (and obvious) problem was that I now owed Steven £400,000. But at least he was a 'civilian' so he wouldn't kill me if I didn't pay him. So, in my own twisted mind, the pressure was off for the moment.

To be fair, it was a real result thanks to Henry when I got the Dubai people off my back, although they did come back again, claiming I owed them more money which was typical of this whole 'game'. You see, no one really wants you to pay them back in full because then you don't need to borrow any more money; the spiral then stops and prevents them from getting rich out of your misery.

At least Henry was able to tell them to back off because the Dubai people were after £20,000 more. They'd tried to warrant their claims by insisting they'd still come after me, even if it was only for £5,000. I said to them, 'You've earned £1 million or more out of me. Leave me alone now. Let me get on with my life.'

With that, they disappeared on me again but there's no guarantee they won't reappear again sometime.

I even got Henry off my payroll for a bit by telling him I didn't want to keep making him look bad by telling people I was going to pay them when I wasn't.

Around the same time – early 2009 – I got a call from a local number and it was the same two Greek lumps who were in the office when I got smashed in the face. They were obviously not happy.

'You owe us the fuckin' money. You fuckin' got to pay it.'

With Henry away having a break, I thought to myself, 'Shit, what do I do now?'

Then I performed one of my typical rabbit-out-of-the-hat tricks: 'I'll give you five grand today.'

Thank goodness they agreed to accept my proposal. They insisted on me going to Finchley Central station where they sent a girl up to me; I had to give the money to her and then off they all went.

I agreed to see them with more money the following week, knowing full well that Henry would be back and hoping he'd deal with them. If it cost me a 'bag of sand' (a grand), as Henry called it, then so be it.

When Henry reappeared, he went with me to meet the Greeks and told them not to worry and I agreed to pay them five grand on the 15th of each month.

So now we were at the end of January 2009, and I seemed to be once again beginning to sort things out, although I also had to find another six grand a month to pay the guy who'd originally introduced me to Henry. Yes – that debt still hadn't been completely paid off. What a mug I must seem at times.

Then, in the middle of all that, Steven started putting me under enormous pressure for that £400,000. I managed to convince a gangster whom I had paid back that there was a fat deal on the table that he might want to get involved in. I told him it totalled £400,000, knowing full well it would give me enough money to pay back Steven and do a final deal with Henry's mates to pay that off as well. If I pulled this off, I would effectively be wiping off £1 million of debt. What a result that would be.

I also managed to convince this gangster to buy the platinum and not sell it until it went up, which effectively bought me a lot more time with which to use his cash. Without it, I wouldn't be able to survive. I needed time almost more than I needed the money at that moment.

But, if this gangster said sell, I'd be in the shit because the truth was I didn't have any platinum to sell. And it wasn't finished there, either. In desperation, I needed to find a buyer, so I flew to Chicago to see a jeweller I knew to set up four meetings. I stayed there for three days. Every meeting was a very formal suit-and-tie affair but no one wanted to supply me with platinum. It turned out to be a complete waste of time.

And there were even more problems when I got back to the UK with that gangster wanting me to sell his platinum, unaware he didn't actually have any. Somehow, I managed to buy myself another two weeks' grace by saying I had sold it but not all the paperwork and stuff had been completed. I was walking an ever-thinning tightrope. But how much longer before I fell off? It was surely only a matter of time.

In April 2009, my money problems caught up with me in a very dramatic fashion yet again. Three black guys turned up on my sister's doorstep asking to speak to me. They left a phone number and, naturally, it completely freaked her out.

I immediately 'recalled' Henry and, for a grand, he phoned these people to find out who they were connected to. That's when I discovered that old debts might fade away but they never fully disappear. It turned out these 'gentlemen' were from that evil bastard Ben and his debt that went back to 2006.

Henry told them I couldn't arrange another loan and said he was going to think about what to do. He also told them that my sister had had problems before with 'visitors' and that she had had CCTV installed, and she'd called the Old Bill after their visit. Henry even had the balls to tell them to 'stay away' from my sister.

The last thing I wanted was someone turning up at my sister's house and causing problems. Thank goodness for Henry, but the ominous thing about what had happened was that it was clear my family were going to be pulled further and further into the hole with me, unless I sorted everything out very quickly.

23

ALL THAT GLISTERS ...

There were other troubling incidents, too. Around this time, I got a phone call from my old GP telling me that someone who had claimed to be from Harrow Hospital had tried to update my records, and they were trying to get my address. The doctor thought it didn't make sense and refused to co-operate, and had the sense to call me and tell me. I had no doubt that one of my creditors was trying to find out where I lived, so they could pay me a visit.

Somehow, I got to Easter 2009 in one piece, without any of these circling predators actually going near my family again. The long bank holiday weekends were always good for me because I got a bit of rest thanks to the extra days. But then the shit really hit the fan yet again. My old mate Lucas started getting on my back for his mate Lee's money, not to mention the money I owed him, too. He'd lost patience with me after years of loyal friendship. I didn't blame him one bit.

Around that same time, I got myself into more trouble. As usual, I was looking around for ways to try to make money and kept being offered yet more supposedly big gold deals. I'd just had an operation on my ankle in hospital when I got a phone call from a guy who wanted a load of gold bought without going to a refinery.

Then I did something I always swore I would never do. I involved Nic directly in my 'business' because I couldn't drive after my surgery, so she took me up to meet this shady character about the so-called 'gold deal'. It was the only time I ever let Nic come into a meeting with me.

I took the risk because I genuinely thought the whole thing would be a complete waste of time. I also wanted her to see the sort of crap I so often had to put up with. She didn't understand much about my business, so this seemed an ideal way to reassure her that it wasn't so dangerous after all.

Rather than leave her sitting in the car, she came into the meeting with me. It was in a hotel in Victoria, in Central London. First, we linked up with our 'protection', two very well-spoken African guys whom I met through my original broker contact. She had introduced me to gold people in the past. She bought and sold sugar and steel, so she didn't know jack shit about this particular 'product', but she begged me to at least test the water with these particular punters – a foxy-looking Russian woman and a younger man who could well have been her son. She looked as hard as nails, like a soulless brothel madam in many ways.

Soon after meeting up, the Russian woman pulled a bullion

bar out of a bag there and then and claimed they had 20 of these bars. She said they had cut them all up into tiny pieces but they couldn't go into a refinery with them because all the bars were stolen. I knew instantly that was a big crock of shit. It didn't make sense. But I knew only too well how easy it would be to transport 20-odd kilos of stolen gold through borders.

The woman and her 'son' showed me the nuggets and there was no way you could use cutters to turn them into nuggets. They were definitely talking rubbish but I wasn't going to tell them that in case all hell broke loose. The only way they could have done what they'd claimed was to re-melt them and then turn them into nuggets.

But I just went with the flow for the moment. They wanted someone to come to the hotel with £150,000 in cash and, once they had seen that cash, they would let me test the gold. Then we would come back, pay them their money and one of their people would hand it over.

I smelled a big rat and so I told them, 'Guys, thank you very much, but this is not for me.'

I was convinced this Russian woman worked for a company and had taken the gold in some kind of dispute. The deal simply wasn't for me and I could see it all ending in tears. It was some kind of scam. As far as I was concerned, it was a non-starter.

But then on the way home with Nic that day, a mate of mine called Steven who lived close by rang me. I told him about my day and what had happened. He immediately said he'd like to do the deal. I was gobsmacked at first. I even said I thought it was a scam but he was convinced there was potentially a huge profit to be made.

'We should just go for it,' he said excitedly down the phone, as Nic drove me, listening intently to every word.

So that's precisely what we did.

I got back in touch with the gold contact through the broker and said I now had a chance to do this deal, so we called that dodgy pair and told them the deal was back on. Steven had agreed he would finance the deal to the tune of £150,000 sterling and then turn that into euros for the actual transaction.

Then I went back to the hotel to show the Russian woman and her 'son' the euros as evidence that we were serious about the deal. We then went outside to a car with the Russian woman and she took a handful of gold out of the bag and put it into a small sample bag.

It all looked and felt right but everything did seem a little too easy for comfort. I just couldn't put my finger on what was wrong so I carried on because it seemed like a fantastic deal, potentially. And remember, I was desperate for cash and I thought this might be a life-saver. I pushed all my suspicions to the back of my mind.

So they gave me the sample bag while the 'son' taped the bag back up and then I went with one of my African bouncers and the 'son' to the refinery in Hatton Garden. There we tested the gold sample they had given us and it was the real thing. So I phoned Steven and he told me to release the money, although he insisted we withhold 30 per cent while we had the rest of the gold tested. I still advised Steven not to go through with it, because something was bothering me, but he insisted, so we went ahead.

We all then got back in the car at the refinery and I gave the 'son' all the money (less 30 per cent) in the back of the car. He counted it all very carefully.

Once he said it was all there, we all headed back towards the hotel. Just before we got to the hotel, the 'son' in the back insisted on getting out to go and put the money away.

So we dropped him off and went on back to the hotel where Steven, our fixer and our other African minder were waiting with the Russian woman. But the problem was she had disappeared before any of us had arrived back. We should have been celebrating with her, but the fact she had gone meant something was seriously wrong. No one else seemed to understand why I was panicking, but I knew from that moment on we'd been done over.

'Hang on. This doesn't make any sense,' I said to the others.

Our two African bodyguards were waiting to be paid their commission, so they looked completely thrown. We took all the so-called gold and left the two Africans still convinced the woman and her 'son' would eventually return. Two hours later, the two black guys rang us to say they were still waiting there. Steven and I laughed about it, although I was still worried something was wrong. None of it made any sense. Why would they leave without their 30 per cent?

The next morning, Steven and I left for the refinery in Hatton Garden at 9.00am. The man in charge still had the original sample bag from the previous day but then the guy inside the bigger bag we'd brought in and picked up the 'gold' and said immediately, 'This isn't real.'

To my eye, it looked exactly the same as the earlier stuff, so I said, 'Don't be silly.'

He replied, 'All right, I'll test it but I tell you it's not real.'

He sounded so sure of himself that I had a horrible feeling he was probably right.

He checked it and, minutes later, announced it was brass. In fact, it turned out to be 20 kilos of brass worth about seven quid. No word of a lie. We had been well and truly fleeced.

Steven broke down in the room and began crying because he had just lost every penny of his investment. I was more worried by the fact I knew he had a terrible temper and, once he flew off the handle, there was no telling what might happen. I also didn't want him thinking I was involved in it. He was the father of my kids' friends after all, not some gangster. We mixed in the same circles and knew a lot of the same people.

Back at the refinery, the man in charge said the other bit of genuine gold they gave us to begin with was worth seven grand, so he paid us it in cash and that was that.

Steven insisted on going to the police, knowing full well that, if I tried to object, then it would make me look even more guilty of involvement. But, perhaps not so surprisingly, the police weren't really *that* interested.

Look at it from their point of view – a bunch of dodgy characters had tried to pull off an iffy gold deal with a bunch of even dodgier foreigners and it had turned effectively into just over a hundred grand robbery in the middle of London. Why should the long arm of the law give a shit?

So, having spoken to the totally uninterested police, Steven and I were driving back home and he was still crying. Now I could have easily pointed out there and then that it was his fault for insisting on doing this deal when I had already thought it was risky. But I thought better of that and decided to get even more involved because we had to stick together on this one and I didn't want him hating me.

So I said to him I'd try to move this scam on to someone else. It was the only chance we had to get some of Steven's money back. He was pretty bemused when I said it at first, but then he started to get the point. We took the brass to the other refinery in Essex and got it all melted down and turned it into a bar. We then got drill samples to make sure there wasn't gold for a second time and there was just a pound's worth of gold like we had before.

I then told Steven I had found someone to do this scam on. He was driving me mad by this time because he'd never really appreciated the risks involved in the first place. After all, he was a 'civilian' and he just didn't understand the rules of the game.

Then (I am sorry to admit this) I did something which sums up the state of my brain when it came to money and my desperate need for it – I borrowed another £30,000 off Steven.

Now, you might rightly think that is one of the most outrageous things I have ever done, considering I had just lost this guy over £100 000. But I obviously did not see it that way. I needed that money to set up the scam which then might help us get some of Steven's cash back, so it all made perfect sense to me.

Luckily, I had these not too clever northerners with whom I was trading a bit of real gold and platinum at the time, and they seemed perfect 'targets'. I said I had a bar of gold for £150,000 and, if they wanted it, they could have it and that it was actually worth about £190,000 on the open market.

It was basically the same scam that had been pulled on us. I told them we had to pay off the £150,000 urgently but then they backed off and said they didn't want the gold after all. It was a major blow. I then had to borrow £30,000 off a mate of mine called Elliot in order to pay that £30,000 back to Steven.

But, more importantly, I now had a major problem with Steven because he'd started accusing me of not trying to get him his money back from the original scam. He just didn't get it and he was becoming more than just a pest, so I had to ask my ex-boxer friend Charles to go and 'have a word' with him. Charles had become a very close friend of mine; we got close very quickly and he could see I was being bullied by people and really did not like it. He was a doorman as well as being an ex-boxer, and he takes no shit from anyone. It was a shame it got to that, really, but Steven gave me no choice.

Charles ended up meeting Steven and telling him to 'stop taking the piss with Jason. Leave him out of this.'

But Steven just didn't get the message. He said, 'He keeps lying to me and lying to me.'

As I pointed out to Steven, 'I am only lying because you keep pressurising me.' I was tempted to scam someone else just to get him his money back, but why should I take that sort of risk for him? He just wouldn't stop harassing me, so I had to keep lying to him to get some breathing space.

Steven had convinced himself I'd sold the gold myself and the cheeky bastard had the front (and stupidity) to say he was going to send a heavy round to get me. I really did not need this sort of aggro from a bloody 'civilian' who was completely out of his depth. The trouble is that Steven had become such a pest I just wanted him out of my life, and his missing money no longer mattered because he had become such a pain in the arse.

Then, in the middle of all this drama with Steven and that gold scam, another character I mentioned earlier called Lee Downs, my good friend Lucas's mate, got on my case for £500,000! I still owed Lucas money, and he was also becoming increasingly agitated with me. I didn't really blame him.

Lee and Lucas started doing a 'good cop, bad cop' routine on me. They were really pissed off with me and they were getting really heavy and threatening. Some nights, I avoided going home in case Lee was hanging around near my house. He was fed up of my lies and I couldn't really blame him one bit. I owed them a shitload of money and I wasn't even paying them any interest. Even though he was my mate, Lucas was becoming a lot harder about everything and he was saying he was going to bring 'some people' round to my house and 'talk' to me, and I'd worked out it would not be nice. The funny thing is, I completely understood his point of view! I just could not handle all the pressure; it was coming from all angles.

So I was back on that familiar treadmill, ducking and diving to keep alive, literally. Just before Easter 2009, I pretended to pay the money back to Lucas's mate Lee, but it was using a forged document. I paid a cheque into Lee's bank account on the Thursday before Easter, so he thought it was a banker's draft. But at least it gave me some peace over the holiday weekend. I'd paid the cheque into the account so they saw the money had gone in and that bought me five days until the cheque bounced.

Meanwhile, I gave Steven £30,000 back, but that only covered what he had lent me after that gold scam was uncovered. He was still thousands of pounds out of pocket.

I did genuinely try to get some of Steven's money back for him. After all, he had been the victim of a scam I'd introduced him to. But he was getting so annoying I was beginning not to bother.

Lucas even admitted he didn't really need the money I owed him, but he and Lee just wanted to make an example of me. The pressure was really being piled on now so I had no choice but to get Henry involved again. At that time, Henry was already paying money to the Birmingham people on my behalf.

Then we got towards May and it dawned on me that I had taken all this as far as I could. All my life I'd always thought there would be another person around the corner to bail me out. It had to stop before I really did lose my life over it.

So I told Henry I had 'a bit of a problem'. I tried to explain to him what had happened and how I came to owe Lee Downs £500,000 and how he wanted to kill me. Henry listened as intently as ever and then said in his own inimitable way, 'Leave it to me, Jason.'

So that's exactly what I did, and Henry phoned Lee and said, 'Hello, Lee, it's me, Henry.'

Henry told me later there was a long pause while Lee absorbed the significance of Henry's involvement in my debt. Then Henry chipped in merrily, 'Let's have a meet regarding Jason.'

So me, Henry and Lee met in the Tesco's car park on the A10. Lee was obviously very twitchy that Henry was going to turn up with an army of heavies but Henry didn't need to flex his muscles. As I've said before, his name was enough to scare the living daylights out of most people.

As Henry stood by, I explained to Lee that it would take a while to get his money sorted out. That was the understatement of the year, even by my standards. Luckily, these people were convinced that, if they did something bad to me, Henry would turn up on their front door. With Henry at the centre of things, my creditors usually gave me that extra bit of time. He was worth his weight in gold.

Anyway, back to reality – I needed £37,500 to pay the rent, school fees and Henry because I was now paying him £5,000 a month to keep people like Lee off my back.

Then I did something outrageous even by my standards. I needed money so desperately I went back to Lee Downs with the same fake bar of gold from earlier and he gave me £37,000 for it. I know ... I know. This sounds like suicide but I'd also offered to get him a watch he wanted. Looking back on it, it was all completely fucking mad, but when you are under extreme pressure you do extreme things.

But the craziest thing of all was that he gave me the £37,000, virtually without questioning it. I did wonder if it was some sort of trick. Let me put it this way – I owed this guy £500,000 and he lent me more cash based on a fake bar of gold. I guess he thought I wouldn't have the bottle to fuck him over again.

Meanwhile, Steven was getting more and more bitter and twisted about the gold deal. In the summer of 2009, he went on holiday with his family after buying up the domain name jasonshifrin.co.uk and jasonshifrin.com and put a website up with a viciously fabricated story of my life. He said I was a convict and even published my wife and children's names, plus my wife's mobile number, my home address, home phone number and some very personal stuff about me. He even included my previous addresses, which was very dangerous for me because it meant anyone who Googled my name would come across the site and could find me with ease.

My wife stumbled upon the website first and immediately called me in tears. We knew it had to be Steven because he had been mouthing off about me for a long time since that scam had gone so disastrously wrong.

I tried to call Steven on his mobile and discovered he was still on holiday in Turkey. Whenever I left a message for him, he just texted me back, saying things like he wanted me to be arrested. He even talked about people going through my bank accounts, and claimed he had a south London face called 'Tom' who would come after me and my family.

Of course, it was all bollocks. Steven knew all along I wasn't involved in losing him his money but he was annoyed that I now wouldn't do something completely illegal. It was as if he just expected me to do his dirty work for him. Steven was still desperate for me to con someone else and recoup his money. In other words, he wanted me to pull the brass trick on a friend.

Eventually, Steven shut down the website but, on the domestic front, Nic refused to have anything to do with Steven's wife and kids after what he'd written about us on that website.

Steven was chasing me for money I did not actually owe him. In fact, he was putting me under more day-to-day pressure than anyone else I owed money to. And I was still having to deal with others, including Lee and Lucas. In the middle of all this, I was being treated by a specialist for an unknown stomach problem. The pressure was finally taking a dreadful toll on my health.

Steven's aggression left me with no choice but to go round and see my heavyweight friend Charles. At one time, he'd run nightclub doors for the top West End clubs. If anyone could sort out Steven, it would be Charles, although I did feel quite bad about having to do this because Steven was completely out of his depth. He should have just swallowed the loss and got on with his life. He never really appreciated how well connected I was and now I felt I had been left with no choice but to have him 'straightened out'.

24

DOUBLE BLUFF

Then suddenly, out of the blue in September 2009, I got word from a contact about another gold deal that sounded virtually identical to the one in which we'd been scammed six months earlier. I decided to pretend I was really interested because I wanted to know more about this so-called 'deal' as there was a lot of unfinished business in relation to what had happened.

Don't ask me why, but I still felt obliged to try to get Steven his money back, despite his awful behaviour towards me and my family. So I called him and said there was a chance I had found the people who'd nicked his money on that fake gold deal.

He was stunned. 'You're joking. You've got be joking,' he said over and over again on the phone.

I told him I was setting up a meeting and he immediately got completely carried away.

'We've got to kidnap them,' said Steven.

I was appalled. This was a guy who, a few months earlier, had been a law-abiding neighbour with a good job and a nice, happy, honest family. It was almost as if, single-handedly, I had turned him into a criminal, or at the very least had unlocked his criminal instincts, albeit not very clever ones. So I said, 'Steve, for fuck's sake, stop talking like this on the phone. Meet me at nine at my house tonight.'

I needed a bit of breathing space because Steven was once again in danger of turning into a bloody liability.

Steven arrived at my place later that night and insisted we got the minders alongside us for protection. He started telling me how he seriously wanted to go to this hotel, wait for these people to turn up again and then kidnap them before driving them round London in the car. Steven's bright idea was then to make them tell us where his stolen money was and keep them in a lock-up warehouse until the money turned up.

I said, 'Great idea, Steve.'

There was a real danger that Steven might try to put his crazy plan into action. I needed to get a grip of the situation. What was my ultimate aim here? I wanted to prove to Steven I had no involvement in the money being stolen in the first place. That was more important to me than anything else.

Anyway, the first stage of this potty plan was to meet with Steven in a café at noon the following day near the hotel on the Edgware Road where I had already arranged to meet the 'gold people' later that afternoon. Steven came charging into the café like an excited, overgrown schoolboy and not really under-standing the more subtle aspects of what we were about to do. The two black guys we had from the original gold meeting six months earlier were also there for our protection, but they were far from impressed, especially when Steven started loudly banging on about 'kidnapping' and doing this and that to these people.

One of the guys even told Steven, 'We're not kidnappers.'

Typically, Steven didn't really know how to respond.

The two guys were reluctant to even go with Steven to the meeting at the hotel because he was behaving like a madman. Steven and I drove off in his Range Rover with the two tough-looking minders hidden out of view in the back of the car. Then Steven did something really sneaky – he called the police and tried to involve them before we even got to the bloody meeting. Well, the minders hiding in the Range Rover went crazy when they heard Steven on the phone as we drove to the hotel.

The police naturally advised us not to go to the hotel for the meeting with the gold scammers. But Steven insisted, so the police actually told us to detain them if it was the same gang of robbers as before. It felt a bit like the Keystone Cops to me, but Steven was so manic by this stage that I couldn't be bothered to argue with him. The police even gave us a crime reference number to use after we dialled 999 if they showed up.

So, now we were in the car with the two black guys trying to calm everything down before we went into the hotel to see if this was the same pair of con artists from before. We decided to sit outside the hotel and wait for them to go in. It seemed sensible.

Then we'd see them first and we could just walk in and detain them, call the police and get them nicked.

We ended up waiting an hour until they turned up, which seemed to give Steven a nervous breakdown, although it didn't surprise me or the black guys one tiny bit. Finally, we spotted the Russian woman walking in with her 'son'. I called them on the mobile: 'I have the man here with the money. We will be there in five minutes.'

Then I walked into the hotel through one entrance completely on my own. One of our black guys stayed by the main entrance, while Steven and the other minder walked in through another door. I then strolled over to their table and gave 'the money' to the guy sitting down; they still hadn't recognised me from that earlier scam.

Suddenly, all the colour drained from her face as it dawned on her.

I spoke first. 'I think you've got something that belongs to me.'

At that moment, our minder grabbed hold of her bag and Steven grabbed the 'son' with her. She immediately started screaming as if we had attacked her. It was really loud and everyone was looking at us as she kicked out at me and all the coffees flew everywhere. All this was happening in the middle of the Hilton Hotel foyer.

Then, all of a sudden, security in the hotel came at us from all directions. The 'son' managed to slip away in the opposite direction but then he was rugby tackled to the ground by the minder. Eventually, security detained both the man and the woman, even though at first they thought we were the baddies.

Luckily, I convinced the hotel security not to let them go until the police arrived. Officers finally turned up and handcuffed both of them. She was still screaming in a foreign language. It turned out she was actually from Romania, but she had a French and a British passport, as well as her Romanian one. And guess what? When they searched her bag, she had 20 kilos of brass with a receipt. Oh, and she had about five grand's worth of real gold in the same sample package. If all that gold had been genuine, it would have had a street value of over £1 million. It turned out that they'd come in that morning on the Eurostar from Paris.

What had happened to Steven? Well, Steven then turned round and said thanks to the two black guys in the most annoying way. They were still furious about what had happened. When we eventually dropped them off later that evening, Steven asked me how much money they should be given.

I said, 'Well, I don't know … what are you thinking of?'

That's when he said £250 quid each.

I was shocked. 'That's not much for five hours' work. It should be a minimum of a grand.'

But Steven clearly had other ideas. 'No, fuck off. That's way too much money.'

In the end, Steven gave them £500 and they were very upset. Steven ended up having a major bust-up with one of them.

Eventually, Steven did send them the rest of their money but my guys were so disgusted they gave him back the money and sent him a professional invoice for £5,000. One of them told me, 'If he wants to be clever, then we'll be clever, too.'

Steven's biggest mistake was not giving those guys the respect they deserved. Respect is a big deal in the underworld. 'Civilians' don't really get that and they never will.

Funnily enough, as we drove home, Steven actually conceded that he'd got me completely wrong. He admitted he'd been unfairly blaming me for all sorts of things, none of which had anything whatsoever to do with me. I suppose I should have been glad to hear him say that, but he'd been such a pain in the arse I wasn't that interested. I just wanted to get shot of him by this time.

Henry wasn't involved in this gold scam at all, but he was still up to his neck with me in the Lee Downs/Lucas £500,000 problem and there were others chasing me as well. It really was a never-ending cycle. Every time I tried to get off, something conspired to stop me. Round and round I went.

Then the shit hit the fan with the Greeks who I had also been paying five grand a month to. They started to get really heavy when it dropped to one or two grand.

Not long after this, I went to a meeting at the home of a guy I was planning to co-promote a white-collar boxing match with. During the meeting, I got loads of heavy phone calls from people I owed money to. The pressure was really getting to me and I couldn't stop sweating, literally. I was on anti-depressants to keep my stomach calm but I was feeling very sick.

By the time I left that meeting, I couldn't even face driving my car. I ended up blacking out in the front seat, luckily before I switched the engine on. I woke up a few hours later in an A&E ward after a heart-attack. I only discovered later that I survived because my friend Charles sped me to the hospital in his car after finding me slumped over my wheel. I ended up staying in hospital for five days before they announced I had made a full recovery.

The first night was a blur: I woke up in the middle of the night on an intensive-care ward and thought I was dead. The next few days I spent reflecting on my life; I thought a lot about my family and friends and then got upset about how fucked up my life had become. It was a very low point; the days felt like weeks and still the phone would ring but it wasn't people calling to see how my health was, it was calls chasing money. The Greeks sent two blokes to my house with an axe to smash Nic's car windows (I have the whole thing on my CCTV). I kept waking up and would think my old friends the Sugars or the Dennis family would walk through the door and say, don't worry, we are here to help, but, of course, it never happened.

Two days after I got out of hospital, Wensley, who I wrote this book with, invited me to his home in Spain to finish the book and have a rest. The Greeks knocked on my front door while I was still away. Nic refused to answer but, obviously, it was very scary for her because I wasn't around at the time. Then, the following day, they phoned to let me know it was them.

The idea was to scare me into paying them a big chunk, but, since I didn't have any money, I wasn't really in a position to respond positively. This was so often the problem. They presumed I always had access to money and, when I failed to cough up, they found it hard to believe I really was penniless.

So I had no choice but to get Henry back to phone them and

tell them we were going to the police and they should never try to intimidate my family again.

I was standing next to good old Henry when he told them, 'You have to give the boy more time.'

'But how much longer does that mean?' came the reply.

'Probably only a few more weeks at the most,' answered Henry.

The other problem was that I couldn't ever seem to finish off making the last couple of repayments on a loan. Something inside me stopped me, because I was always looking for another deal to secure. Maybe it was also just too easy and I thrived on the drama?

Now, that might sound twisted but there may be some truth in it. Let me explain: I am a natural deal-maker, so, once I've sorted out most of a debt, I naturally ease off because I am now out looking for fresh funding.

But here's the even more twisted part: I quite like keeping these gangsters on a lead because, while they are not being paid, I have a little bit of power over them. They won't turn on you until they get their money. Isn't that ridiculous?

But it's true.

Of course, on the other side of the coin, it was nice to get rid of these debts and it was always such a relief to wipe the slate clean, but there was always someone else I owed money to. For example, the Lee Downs £500,000 would never go away. I still get texts and phone calls to this day. Every now and again, I try to calm him with a gesture, such as going to a jeweller I know and buying a watch for £20,000 and giving it to Lee, just as a peace token. It always worked for a few days and that would make me feel better, but it didn't make any of the debts go away. I was going to have to drip-feed back the money to these people one day. There was no way to escape it.

And, of course, I was still digging myself further and further into the hole. Sometimes, like I did with Lee, I'd come up with a short-term 'fix' by getting hold of a watch and giving it to my creditor to try to calm things down. It usually worked well because it might get me a few weeks' breathing space.

But those little 'breathers' didn't last long. All of a sudden, the gangster would demand that I had to pay up. I gave one civilian I'd borrowed ten grand from a cheque that bounced. He went ballistic at me and said he was going to expose me on Facebook if I didn't pay him. So I urgently had to find a way to borrow more money to pay for that.

And so the vicious circle went on and on and on. I now needed another deal to get myself out of this latest crisis. The only way was to earn some money.

In the middle of all this, I started to buy and sell watches again, as well as brokering gold and silver deals.

Throughout 2009, there were numerous, heart-stopping moments when I thought, 'Fuck! Have I gone too far this time?'

The police continued to be a bit unhelpful. And strangely, whenever they knew where I actually lived, I'd get a visit from a crim shortly afterwards. That's a bit of a coincidence, isn't it?

Once, Henry called and said, 'Listen, Jay. Someone just phoned me to say they know where you live.'

The same people even told Henry I was at a very important Jewish festival. They even said what house I'd gone to and who I was with. That was quite chilling.

Henry warned me that they really meant business when they went to these sorts of lengths. He said, 'You must start paying some money because they're on to you now.'

I said, 'What do you mean?'

And that's when he revealed to me that I was being followed everywhere I went. 'And then they followed you home, mate,' he explained.

I hadn't even noticed.

AFTERWORD

It's now 2011 and I still owe money to all sorts of shady characters. It's tough out there. The current precarious economic climate means that it's even harder to find anyone prepared to invest in new projects. I am only just managing to keep my head above water by taking advantage of the way that people today are desperate to see off their old gold.

On the domestic front, it's not been easy, either. When my uncle suddenly died recently, I discovered that, despite thinking we got on well, he didn't really like me. I think it all went back to issues he had with my mother when they were kids. But his death was a tragedy, and he will be missed.

In the summer of 2010, my cousin Elliot was diagnosed with bone cancer. I took him to see a knee specialist and was in the room with him when he heard the news. He broke down in floods of tears and so I tried to support him and get his life back into

shape so he could fight it with all his strength. This will sound sick but, in some ways, I was jealous of him because at least he could sit down and plan out his life now because he knew how long he had to live. He eventually had his main operation in May 2010, and he seems to be making a good recovery, so hopefully he may have turned the corner in terms of his treatment.

Meanwhile, Nic and I continue to move house with alarming regularity. It's a horrible way to live but we seem to have no choice. My wife's loyalty towards me is remarkable. I don't deserve it at all since I am still putting her through hell.

Our closest friends continue to be rocks of support, even at the most deadly of moments. I can never thank them enough for all the loyal support they have shown us in recent years. It is more than words can describe.

There is no right way to end this book as things are constantly changing. Even as I write these words, there are certain gangsters after me. Obviously, I'd like to end this painful chapter in my life by turning this book into a big success. But, more importantly, if my book ends up preventing just one person from falling into the same financial mess as me, then it will all have been worthwhile.

So there you have it. My crazy life ducking and diving round some of the nastiest criminals you are ever likely to meet. It's been one hell of a ride and, unfortunately for me, it's not over yet. Because, as you've probably noticed, they are still chasing me. I've written this book in the hope it will help me out of that awful hole, which has brought me so close to death and self-destruction.

At certain moments, I've even convinced myself that revealing

the murky world of money-lending and the evil characters who operate within it might help protect me in some twisted sort of way. One old crim I came across a few years ago said that the best way to avoid being knocked off by another criminal was to 'go public, because no self-respecting hit-man would ever kill a target if he thought his crime might be splashed across the front pages'.

Hopefully, he's right. Hit-men thrive on anonymity and usually their crimes end up in what the media calls a 'filler' paragraph buried well inside the newspaper so that no one takes much notice. But it would be foolhardy of me to rely on imagined fame preventing my premature death.

So here I am, still on so many gangsters' wanted lists. Obviously, my biggest problem is that, until I have cleared all those so-called debts, the pressure continues to mount. Now, many of you reading my story would rightly expect a book like mine to have a nice, neat ending. But you're in for the ultimate surprise ending with my story because not even I know what is going to happen.

Even as I write this, I am still looking over my shoulder, wondering who is going to turn up on my doorstep next or what that car is doing following me or whether my old protector Henry Carter can actually come to my rescue yet again.

The police are not interested, because their attitude – understandably, to a certain degree – is that, if I get 'popped', it's just another one of 'them' off the streets. But that's mightily unfair because I am not even a criminal, in any real sense of the word. I'm just a regular guy who got sucked into borrowing money in order